The Long Overdue Letter

by Dinah Chapman Dubble

PublishAmerica
Baltimore

© 2009 by Dinah Chapman Dubble.
All rights reserved. No part of this book may be reproduced, stored in a retrieval system or transmitted in any form or by any means without the prior written permission of the publishers, except by a reviewer who may quote brief passages in a review to be printed in a newspaper, magazine or journal.

First printing

PublishAmerica has allowed this work to remain exactly as the author intended, verbatim, without editorial input.

ISBN: 1-60703-990-7
PUBLISHED BY PUBLISHAMERICA, LLLP
www.publishamerica.com
Baltimore

Printed in the United States of America

To the children:
May all find a mother like mine!

Acknowledgement Is to a Mother's Love:

ANNA ELIZABETH MOYER

April 30, 1915 to January 17, 2008

I entirely credit my Mother for the thoughts contained in *The Long Overdue Letter*.

Through her love
A silent understanding
Guided my way.

The Long Overdue Letter

Introduction

This concise work suggests the factor responsible for the ascent of mankind is not our likeness to the apes,—but to God!

Suggests it may not be wise to discard the testimony of uncounted millions who found identity through prayer. Because not natural physical;—but spiritual adaptation seems the vector of progress.

The human course seems guided by common emotional needs. Personal expectations described in words as truth, freedom, equality, compassion, peace, personal talent fulfillment and everlasting life. These have been the navigators toward a state of environmental compatibility,—or JUSTICE.

An invisible strength identified as the "human spirit" emerges when these needs are oppressed. No power on earth,—not the Romans, the Saracens, the British, the Confederates or the Nazi Regime could annihilate this energy source.

America is more than a geographic location. It is a dream that lives in the heart of everyone. Words as freedom, truth or justice defy academic definition. Still,—to satisfy these needs has been our goal.

That these common needs surround all social reform,—may

identify this composite of human ideals as an inherent social conscience. We focus on physical attributes oblivious to the ethereal nature of the person and this conscious component.

That an organism be compatible with its environment is a basic biological principle. Of one thing we can be certain. The cave men were definitely not where they wanted to be! All human direction is toward emotional satisfaction and comfort. Progress is in essence an effect of environmental incompatibility. The origin of humanity then should trace to a compatible place. We are not satisfied with temporary comfort, but seek everlasting well-being. So our beginning then should trace to a land before time, a pre-evolution 'mother earth'.

Everything we perceive is relative to an already existent entity; transmissions happen only at a present point in time; and our progress is only an awareness and utilization of principles that always existed. The 'heaven' we seek may be a vestigial memory of the stable everlasting world we came from; and not be some distant place. But exist right in our midst, with separation from this world being only of a conscious nature.

Survival of the most fit, in the case of humanity has not flowed with the most powerful;—but the searchers for TRUTH and believers in JUSTICE!

Answer to the enigma of life may not be buried in the paleontology pit,—but can be discovered—
DEEP IN THOUGHT!

Deep in Thought

To my family,

One evening as loneliness began to encompass my being, I sought solace in the sunset. Reflections emerged which continue to dance in my mind. They compose the message in this long overdue letter. It springs from a burning desire to heal the wounds of our separation.

The still of dusk seemed to direct my focus somewhere inside, where a seed of knowledge began to flourish. Doors opened to expose a view surpassing the splendor of the fading scenery. Although conditioned to look outside for answers; that night instead proved insight my most prized possession. We examine rocks from outer space; and dig in the paleontology pit; but the treasure may be buried deep in thought.

Diversification in our world is determined by nuclear components. And throughout the protoplasmic structure whispers a voice of harmony. This natural arrangement allows no exception to the rule. Herein lies our peculiarity. Where nature provides other species with immediate environmental knowledge; we instead tediously move toward realization. Environmental truths, or physical principles escape detection by our physical sensory mechanisms. As was our harmonious nature, our capacity to love, long buried under physical perceptions of social conflicts and performances. A perceptive ability beyond the physical view moved us from a flat to a global world, and from conflict to compatibility. Truths sporadically arrived from, and are realized within a common place deep in thought. Almost suggesting humanity sustained a deep psychological wound, and progress merely a recovery!

As a contemplative move carried me into the night, the brilliance of the moonlit sky transformed from its chemical composure. The view was replaced by considerations of American colonists and our founding fathers. Before scientists penetrated the appearance of planet earth, our ancestors seem to have identified natural laws. They were instrumental in designing a government in likeness to the ecological arrangement. In fact, American democracy resembles the intrinsic structure of all life forms. Where individual cells contribute a particular function to organs, which contribute functions to systems—which interrelate harmoniously to form a whole. That we became prolific should not be an enigma! When the American Liberty Bell rang, a natural proclivity to succeed may have been released.

A biological overview shows humanity may be the only species where mental formation and behavior can be extremely variable, and tends to be acquired from the environment. This outside-in process seems an anomaly that should not exist in the highest rung of the biological evolutionary hierarchy ladder. Physiological composition directs a uniform behavior in other species. Energy flows from the inside-out! Before America came into existence, outside sovereign ruling powers not only formed, but controlled human thought and activity. American founders reversed this system, arranged a government comparable to, and compatible with the overall scheme. After individuals had just a scintilla of release from oppression, and the basic format copied by other nations, an acceleration of progress transpired like never before.

Not our linear dimensions divide us, but our ideology. There seems to be a purpose for everything in the world we live. It is vital for individual members to contribute specialized functions for support of the whole. Each eco-system has been classified as to structure and function. Separate areas of activity obey specific laws. Survival of the whole is dependent on individual specialization. Structure demands stability of conditions, and therefore a natural conformity is provided. Instinctive compliance to a natural order secures harmonious inter-relationships. No member of any group, except the human race seems capable of forming a separate ideology. A 'free will' seems purely the human privilege. But, it is one in which the manner of exercise becomes a crucial factor in the determination of our destiny.

"We hold these truths to be self-evident, that all men are created equal, that they are endowed by their Creator with certain unalienable Rights, that among these are Life, Liberty and the pursuit of Happiness."—This excerpt from the Declaration of Independence suggests humanity also holds a common set of behavioral rights,—a natural social conscience. It seems the nature of our success should prove this to be correct and lead to the restoration of humanity to a natural state. Unfortunately where our remarkable progress and accumulation of scientific knowledge should reinforce the validity, it still today goes unrecognized.

Our motto E. Pluribus Unum, one out of many, reflects the manner of diversification in nature. The image incorporated into social government worked. To sustain life seems the end product of the machine we call planet earth. Justice would be the end product of the social machine called the United States of America! Our road to justice seems to have been determined by conscious, or attitude changes. Common ideals have been the permanent conscious energies directing our course throughout all the changing eras. We hold a common inherent ideology described in words as: love, equality, freedom, truth, peace, personal worth and everlasting life. Satisfaction of these human needs during social exchange establishes a conscious state of happiness, or justice! This human moral inclination was oppressed by religious and social power control systems. The American gift was freedom to satisfy these everlasting inherent desires! To comply with this direction seems vital. Unity through this seemingly natural common ideology may be more involved than a means to establish personal satisfaction, or happiness. Justice may be an ecological demand!

The banner for justice was carried forward throughout all the eras. Despite cruel reception and punishment, this idea flowing from the heart of humanity continued to flourish. Overwhelming social powers at times cause the bearers to stumble and fall. But they rise again with what seems supernatural strength. The Believers persevere and gain even more momentum during the 20th Century.

The American Declaration of Independence clearly expresses credence in God given inalienable rights! The framework of the American Constitution seems a support system for these behavioral rights. Thus, our constitution held an open door for human rights activists to enter. Eventual success allowed more of what were considered "self-evident" rights by our forefathers to be recognized, expanded and incorporated into civil law.

Flowing with this influx of moral rights during the last century was a long buried personal ability. Mankind by physical nature adapts to the mind of parents, community, religion and government. That civil rights laws are compatible with a deeper inherent personal nature should be evident by the response. Once the laws were instated, resistance dwindled and social attitudes changed. Suggesting equality to be the truth, and further supported by the eruption of human ingenuity that followed! Could we even imagine the effect a United Nations based on recognition and enforcement of God given 'inalienable rights' would have?

The American Constitution seems a work of art! Composed of not literal steadfast rules, but is an open door toward unlimited actualities. Common ideals as equality, truth or freedom radiate from all social reform, and direction toward common welfare. The words made a difference. Reservations on the journey toward fulfillment of the dream were unlimited. People embarked in increasing numbers. The mighty oak expresses culmination of the acorn, but the fruits of the tree of life seem yet to be realized.

The accuracy of an initial belief in personal worth led to an increased respect for academic education. A cool wind began to blow as I pondered on circumstances that followed. Educational instruction moved primary focus from character development through prayer, to the physical world. As our vision of the physical world expands, the image of God dims. We acknowledge natural intellectual potential, but no longer give any educational billing to nature's God. We develop the intellectual machine, but seem to bury personal talent. Identity of the nature of personal worth, supported by our Constitution began to fade. Other countries and the United Nations copied the governing format, but seemed to lose sight of the energy source. A chill began to permeate my being. Consideration if this altered course could inhibit cultivation of the dream became my dilemma.

Defeat of the anti-war, anti-materialism, anti-conformity and anti-establishment movements in the nineteen sixties seems contrary to a prior overall pattern of ascension toward social compatibility. These ideas seem to express the epitome of all prior social reform effort. Consideration of why the love and peace movement was never able to gain the respect necessary for public support seemed vital to me. Why is it that the believers in justice sit by the wayside, seeming to have lost direction? Did events of the sixties cause a spiritual paralysis, a relapse in the psychological recovery of humanity? Honored leaders as John and Bobby Kennedy, Martin Luther King, and a God of love, the most revered of the people,—were all assassinated! As the business skyscraper began to overshadow the Church steeple, the exact opposite attitudes from the sixties protestors gain power.

The effects of our scientific progress are visible. Awed by technology, we may have overlooked a less tangible attitude change. As public education directed minds toward environmental knowledge, we can sense a gradual loss of love. This loss becomes evident in modern art, architecture, music and morality. Appeal moves from the heart, to the intellect. We move toward a future world depicted by science fiction authors. This future world is a place where vicious predators threaten humanity. Authority becomes determined by victory in technological space wars. Power control reigns through weapons of mass destruction. This future world seems an opposition to the place our ancestors were guiding us. The American dream is a place of fairness, of justice. We were headed for an ideal world. A place where equality, truth, freedom, peace, love, a respect for life and personal talent determine environmental conditions. Before we continue our giant leap into outer space, we may need to consider whether our present route in actuality returns us to the old world from which our ancestors tried to escape. Science fiction movies seem only far more sophisticated and grotesque images of old world activity.

Now, I tend to agree with Marianne Williamson, in that "A Return to Love" is vital to our future success and happiness. However at this stage of development, where education has focused on the world that meets our eyes, I do not believe there is any hope of restoring faith in the traditional manner, or in the emerging contemporary styles. I believe only intellectual prowess directed toward establishing the academic truth of God's existence can evoke our return to love. Just as all other environmental truths existed separate from our awareness, so may God escape detection by our physical sensory mechanisms. For whatever reason, I felt I had to find evidence for my personal resolution to the suspicion in the sixties humanity took a wrong turn on the road to justice.

Then, the following quote by Jonathan Swift came to mind. "I no more believe that the universe was formed by a fortuitous concourse of atoms, than that the accidental jumbling of the alphabet could form a most ingenious treatise of philosophy." Before long I found myself relating this idea to the manner in which the government of The United States of America was arranged. Could it have been mere chance that the formula for the most successful government system resembles the basic structure of planet earth; of all life? In fact, all man made machines are constructed in this manner. Where separate parts are assigned a task, to contribute to a unit, to in turn contribute to a system; which inter-relate harmoniously to form a whole. Do not all machines have a creator? Is this similarity in creative style to that of the biological machines coincidence, or suggest human likeness to a greater creator? Do not all machines have an energy source? Was ours not an indefinable entity called the 'human spirit'? Did it not flow out from deep within personal consciousness? Was it not initiated by a people who prayed? Could the source of self, the life of our body, and our world not be God?

I returned to thoughts of our Declaration of independence. "—To assume among the powers of the earth, the separate and equal station to which the laws of Nature and Nature's God entitle them." I began to ponder on the positive direction effected by increased personal freedoms, and relaxation of social discrimination. Oppression was clearly inhibitory to the release of personal potential. I wanted to determine whether natural ingenuity alone determined our course, or indeed as inferred by our founders, were laws of nature's God involved? It seemed something more than human intellectual abilities must exist. Environmental truths, or knowledge of the biological mechanisms existed before we became aware of it. The only place knowledge can exist is in a mind. So a greater mind should have existed before that of humanity.

Our ascent hardly just naturally fell into place. The majority of human existence is one of pain, suffering and conflict. Then, within the last century comes an astounding alleviation. Overall direction is toward improved communication, and protection from the predatory, or harmful effects of natural events. Were we purely organic creatures we should simply adapt to the predatory motion in the physical world like all other animals. Actually, this apparent desire and capacity to escape from predatory behavior seems a human distinction. As does the manner in which we escape. Physical principles are not visible to the eye, but realized deep in thought. Beyond superior intellectual ability exists a distinction in overall conscious capacity, especially depth perception. This capacity to realize knowledge beyond the world acquired through physical senses seems purely a human trait. If

American success were solely related to release of human ingenuity, why didn't the democratic format work as well for Greece, or when copied later by other countries? Or why did other ingenious systems as Nazism, Communism or Fascism fail?

I then gave some thought to "the separate but equal station." Each person is separate, the center of his/her own world. Each person has equal expectations from social exchange. Comes equipped with an inherent moral code. Each person wants to feel equal, to be loved, to be at peace with others, expects honesty, wants to fulfill a personal talent,—and so on. Recognition of this "separate, but equal station" may have been what made the American difference. The freedom extended in America was to a personal, but common natural behavioral consciousness. It almost seems as though our founders essentially gave the age old Golden Rule national recognition.

American success should validate the Golden Rule's authenticity. Today, the Golden Rule comprehensible to our founders defies academic definition. As do the entities as equality, freedom, truth or justice, that make it work. Then I began to ponder on the fact that everything in the human mind has a real source. Everything we tend to credit to human imagination is a copy of a geometric design, physical principle or form already in existence. And everything we engineer follows an already present overall natural pattern. Therefore so should these moral ideas have a real source. The ideals America was founded on have no physical characteristics! Could their existence within thought suggest our perceptive ability goes beyond the world to which we are physiologically adapted? To a world unlike our reality based on time and distance? Because where our intellectual reality changes, the desire for truth and justice has been an everlasting presence throughout all the eras. Truths, and our ability to realize them was always present, just occult, buried under a mind that was wrong. That as the error was caused by an illusion, or the appearance of things; so may be the appearance human intellect alone is responsible for progress. Most especially because the Golden Rule, words as freedom or justice; the word truth itself defies intellectual comprehension.

There seemed to me an urgency to solve the dilemma as to the rightness of our present direction. The social route we began after the sixties began to seem like only a structure transfer from a simulation of the appearance of things; to a simulation of the intrinsic physical arrangement. The ancient mind formed by environmental appearance, brought an oppressive reality into existence; the Colonial American mind opened an opportunity for the people to bring an ideal reality, a place of 'fairness' into existence; the scientific mind formed by the biological machine, brings a mechanical, or robotic reality,—a social machine into existence. The human body automatically delivers an image to the person; and the person copies what it sees. Unlike other life forms guided by an intrinsic knowledge, the human is guided by extrinsic instruction. The knowledge introduced by scientists was factual, supported by concrete evidence. Academia began to focus on these environmental truths. It stands to reason then, the transfer of thought to physical structure, or scientific progress caused a steady downfall in religious faith, as God is not visible. In addition scientific evidence conflicted with religious views. The concept of God was removed from public education and media on the basis of the 1st Amendment, which was added to our Constitution to ensure personal freedoms. This dismissal of God from social affairs also seems relative to the transition to linear thought. God, an entirely personal conscious experience viewed through the growing linear perspective, acquired a material form called religion. And so "Congress shall make no law respecting an establishment of religion" became applicable. It seemed to me, where science boasts 'truth', it did not disprove the existence of God. To consider the strong human emotional attachment to God ever since cave days, and the credence of our finders in what were considered natural laws of God; this burial did not seem wise.

Scientists seemed to accept the complex intrinsic natural arrangement as a fortuitous circumstance. Religions believed it to be evidence of "intelligent design" by nature's God. To me, neither seemed right. It seemed contrary to reason to suspect the complex and seemingly purposeful natural inter-relationship did not have a conscious source. But on the other hand, intelligence is an organic function, a brain function. Would only be a piece of the whole machine,—of the Creation; only a means for an animal to comprehend the environment. The more I thought about a God with a human brain, the more ludicrous the idea became. There must be another explanation. I began to consider the manner steadfast laws govern the physical world; and again the way mankind seemed to copy this natural arrangement, or incorporate it into a social judicial system,—or manmade laws. And the manner both manmade mechanical and political machines in likeness to physical structure, where each unit has an assigned task to contribute to a system,—and so on, to form the whole; like the organism they simulate,—are only temporary existences. Why does the highest life form on earth have to copy, to receive instruction from the outside; when every other living organism is equipped with an intrinsic knowledge of their environment?

Then it occurred to me that the technological marvels and intellectual ability we so revere flowed with a steady increase in personal freedom; in essence from people who adhered to personal convictions. The American Liberty Bell gave freedom to personal insight, to a common conscious sense. The contributions that expanded our reality were authentic, came from an inner personal vision. So did the social changes toward equality, peace and compassion. These behaviors were not acquired from the outside environment, but were an opposition to the 'old world' oppressive mentality. This could suggest we too have an intrinsic guidance system, should not have to copy everything. As this inner mind has no physical characteristics, it could be our 'God-given mind; and God may have brought us into existence, just not in any physical manner of creation. Our present course has expanded individual opportunity for education, but fails to nurture personal character. We seem to recognize our strength came from within, but not the energy source. When America was founded, God was the center of social life. Words as devotion, Divine inspiration and honor accompanied progress. Our Declaration of Independence ends with: "And for the support of this Declaration, with a firm reliance on the protection of divine Providence, we mutually pledge to each other our Lives, our Fortunes and our sacred Honor."

With faith in God as their guide these great men envisioned a government system that restored humanity to a natural order. America did not extend total freedom. Our laws do not allow oppression in any degree. The judicial system expanded from covering only physical harms, to include coercive actions of religious and secular organizations. The American difference was freedom to follow your heart or a common ideology as it was considered a God-given right. The desire for truth, freedom, equality, compassion, peace, recognition of personal worth, everlasting life and happiness, or Justice! This ideology could well have been the invisible "melting pot" where variable cultural ingredients unknowingly simmered into a congruent blend of ingenuity and prosperity!

Every species in nature expresses similarity in behavior. Recognition of need for happiness, or justice reduced human division, and restored us to the overall natural scheme by releasing identity of an inherent behavioral philosophy in humanity as well. The American opportunity for the people to pursue happiness, and establish justice released environmental truths and creativity. I then began to give more consideration to the manner these truths became, and continue to be realized.

Unlike the structured and organized laws of nature, these conscious perceptions arrived spontaneously, sporadically and without regard to physical, professional or social status. A geometric design, or physical principle became an idea in someone's mind. Who became devoted to clearing the image, and validate its environmental existence. When satisfied, the idea was presented to an established authority. Where the idea most likely was rejected. And the person ridiculed. Others slowly started to consider the suggestion not immediately accessible through either the physical senses, or reality of the point in time. Eventually the truth was realized and accepted. Then communicated through the educational system. Where the same perceptive process transpires. More than memorization and repetition are required to realize truths. We see what our mind focuses on. Eyes do not see, vision occurs within the 'self'. Intense concentration may be required for the student to realize truth, because it is visible only deep within personal thought.

The manner these truths arrived could be similar to the way people experience the presence of God through personal prayer. Uncounted millions of people have testified to this experience. The same mental process could be applicable. Where the scientist's experience is considered truth, the religious experience is considered mystical. The only difference may be that the scientist's idea has a physical source, where the religious experience is entirely a conscious exchange. Instead of idea to an already existent substance; it is idea to an already existent real idea, or consciousness. The effects of religious experiences are consistently described in words as love or peace; a feeling of inner strength, to have received guidance, protection, freedom from pain; or even physical effects as healing, or an idea from out of the blue that saved a life, or prevented catastrophe. Our social exchange involves more than words. Like the invisible energy allowing the transmission of sound, we sense certain character traits.

We have personal idea to already existent idea experiences, or conscious transfers every day. Communication beyond words, or intellectual discourse transpires during social exchange. A sense of truth, trust or distrust; love or hatred; peace or conflict; equality, freedom or power control; of honor emerges during or after conversation. We leave another person with a good or bad feeling! American RIGHTS, or IDEALS are representations of conscious senses, or social transfers necessary to evoke 'good' feelings, or HAPPINESS.

It seemed to me that common sense consideration of this mental process related to an overview of the human course could add authenticity to the religious view that we were created. With scientific study on our side, we can assume that like we as infants enter an already existent world; so did humanity. Theory suggests that from a rudimentary beginning we evolved to complex intellectual creatures of mother earth. Within the past century, we began to focus on this theory. While it offers truth of physical changes in animals, we may overlook more occult conscious distinctions in humanity. The intellect is a product of the brain, provides the necessary mechanics for physical adaptation. Holding the highest rung on the evolutionary ladder should simply establish humanity as supreme predators. Our interspecies conflict goes beyond a territorial domination necessary for physical survival as identified in other animals. Our history shows periodic invasive human empires express desire to have ultimate power over the world. This seems to suggest that nature intended for the whole planet to be man's territory. However, although we reign supreme over other animals, to fight each other for ultimate power seems to stem from something other than biological engineering. The direction of humanity is to escape from oppression, suggesting in actuality this lifestyle is incompatible.

Words as truth, freedom, equality, love, peace, personal worth and a right to enjoy life became the way. Justice,—the destination. An unspoken message of religious teaching,—the compass. How to be a better person,—the primary education. These common ideals brought America into existence. America is more than a geographic location. When the American Liberty Bell rang, it was not the mind or body of the colonists,—but an energy buried deep in the heart of humanity that was released. It was cultivation and release of common aesthetic experiences and abstract images deep in personal thought that brought us to life.

Everything in the human mind has a REAL source. A little child copies actions in the immediate environment. And we continue the process as adults. Be it through formal education, reading or social activity; we continuously acquire knowledge about what already exists. New members of a group will conform to its behavioral style. This is evident in occupation, profession, religion, culture or organization. Most evident in different accents, or languages in groups separated by geographic location. We seem to be automatic copy machines! Where other biological groups are programmed by nature with a specific behavior,—we copy! It seems like America interrupted this habit. Increasing numbers of people became sincere and authentic. Progress is an art. Knowledge is introduced to human reality as though from another dimension. We can see scientific knowledge is based on environmental truths; is not a copy of another person's idea, but actual physical principles. Then also our 'inner' personal knowledge that we call morality, or common decency should also be considered based on a natural conscious truth; most especially because it is not something that can be copied, but only understood within. Should not in the same manner a scientific truth has a physical source, a moral truth have a conscious source,—and that source be the entity we call God?

"We hold these truths to be self-evident that all men are created equal, that they are endowed by their Creator with certain inalienable Rights, that among these are Life, Liberty and the pursuit of Happiness.—

That to secure these rights, governments are instituted among Men, deriving their just powers from the consent of the governed.—."

I then began to consider the thought of self-evident rights, and that governments are necessary for their procurement. Unless humanity also has a common behavior, or does have behavioral rights, it should not matter what style is copied. To reflect on the course of human behavior, it is evident nothing mattered more. Individuals clearly expressed an affinity for the moral principles of personal worth and freedom when they embarked for this 'new world' in massive numbers. Ancient civilizations all express an overall hierarchy system with a master-slave theme. The image extended beyond the physical world to include supernatural gods. One god had ultimate power over the others. This social arrangement could be construed as an automatic copy of the appearance and motion in our physical environment. A mental picture of a place where the more powerful animals tend to devour the weaker; and where natural events as floods, tornadoes or earthquakes overpower all life is delivered to an individual through body mechanics.

Direction away from this predatory behavioral style seems relative to the existence of a carpenter, who walked around the countryside talking to people about love. Christ had a behavioral impact on the world like no other social, religious, political or philosophical treatise to date! Jesus exemplified human potential for a behavior in opposition to the master-slave, or predatory mind of that era. He projected a new image of God as a loving Father! The lessons were not linear, but representations of a greater love and strength. There were no concrete laws or rituals to memorize and repeat. Explanations of the Father's nature were often given in parables. The impact was emotional,—realized deep within each invisible person,—or SELF! From this common place deep in personal thought emerged ideals as equality, freedom, peace and compassion. A respect for personal worth, and a journey toward happiness happened after vision was diverted from the surface to this place deep in thought!

Jesus was a human being, a physical form who treated other people in a manner that evoked a common conscious sense of fairness, and responsibility for the welfare of another person. The beginning of freedom from an oppressive mentality, and awareness a compatible social reality is dependent on release of "self-evident" rights as equality, freedom or peace may well trace to this source. Where else are these inherent conscious needs better exemplified; and where else if not from God, did this conscious sense of fairness come from?

It may be difficult, if not almost impossible to visualize this deeper image through a mind that is formed by literal Biblical interpretation and rigid religious training. Religions have primitive roots, trace to cave dwellings; to a very oppressive reality. All seem to have fitted God into the reality created by mankind. Where Jesus removed the physical garments; the physical mind, ideologies that separate individuals from each other, and individuals from God; religions did not! The message of Jesus is composed of words belonging to an unspoken language, a conscious sense understood by all people. We understand compassion, equality and peace. Is this not the same message of Buddhism, Hinduism or Islam? It would seem that what is experienced only as a conscious sense is our true language. Communication of human behavioral ideals through religions seems understood, and has been the advice most consistent and appreciated by people throughout all the eras. Even in this technological era, the WORD, or love is considered to be 'the way'. At the end of the day our emotional state, our happiness is entirely dependent on the manner this conscious connection with other people is affected; and whether we have been free to express our talent, feel we've done a good job. As in the case of prayer to God, it is an entirely personal experience. So, it would seem then, our individualism can be found here, within personal character; in the personal conscious experience separate from the environmental mind delivered by the physical senses and experienced by all people. A dozen people in an immediate environment will share the same mental picture, but each experience is personal. Where it is noted individualism is the source of progress, and the inhibitory factor to release of its expression is totalitarian control beginning with parents; the exact nature may go unrecognized.

Individuality is an equal natural circumstance. To be an individual is to be free. A physical mind can't be free. Because it seems only a mechanical reproduction, a copy of something. So will always be bonded to its source. The physical mind, body and environment seem to be parts of one interconnected mechanism. Only a 'person' can be free, can have a personal interpretation and response to an environmental thought formed by the brain, to decipher if opinion or truth, choose to retain or discard the thought. A person can become free from even physical disability, find alternate ways of self-expression; as well as from a mind causing fear, hatred or pain.

There is so much inference today that people are biological machines. Discussion about brains, neuro-chemical reactions and electrical impulses that I begin to wonder if maybe I am an anomaly, if nature didn't put me together right! I am not a body. I am not a physical organ, or organism. I am a 'consciousness', a conscious awareness of existence. Perceptions are delivered to 'me', through body mechanics. Very much alive, the 'I' of my body can add perspective, reason and filter the material presented. My eyes do not see,—my brain does not see,—vision occurs within my consciousness,—within my SELF! My 'I' is unique. And there seems no human explanation as to why I, in particular, exist. My body expresses its needs to 'me', to personal consciousness. And through 'me', or consciousness actions emerge toward fulfillment. Unlike the promotion today of need to depend on 'outside' authority and government, I seem put together by nature in a manner that demands self-discipline and personal responsibility. I have a need for entities as love and fairness. These are as abstract as 'I am'. There is no concrete definition or means to provide these needs, so I am told such a world will never happen. Likewise there is no scientific formula to describe the composition of 'me', or consciousness. We do not understand the conscious vessel of awareness through which needs flow. Still I know that I exist;—that I AM. And the nature that endowed me with a basic need for happiness should also hold a means for fulfillment. The potential for JUSTICE must be as real as I am.

Most likely the reason laws, or a judicial system came into

existence was the barbaric behavior of primitive individuals. This memory could be a prognostication of the deleterious impact physical freedom separate from educational means to guide individuals toward self-awareness holds. It may not have been the physical discipline and punishment alone that moved people toward compatible behavior, but the gradual change to laws compatible with the heart of humanity. The emergence of laws to support personal, or self-expression that began in western civilization instead may be what guided us toward truth, compatibility and prosperity. This event was preceded and accompanied by the story of Jesus, the Bible, monasteries, convents and religious retreats and most of all social focus on early childhood instruction to receive guidance from a God of love through personal prayer; on how to be a better person. All of these can transfer vision from the physical mind, or environmental view to a place deep within personal thought. Jesus clearly was free from the oppressive mentality of his era; the Bible constantly warns not to be influenced by the environment.

We can see when minds were formed by the physical environment, behavior was oppressive; the approximate two hundred year period after America came into existence released an occult individualism, which brought forth an awesome ascent, and compatible behavior through a deeper personal reasoning ability. Now since minds have been formed more by academia, than personal prayer, behavior becomes robotic. The fervor surrounding human ideals diminishes. The RIGHTS our country is based on are not understood; all is based on literal and linear interpretation. There is no physical freedom. Everything is inter-related. The physical mind is dependent on a brain, chemistry and environment; is a reflection of something out there. Individualism seems a state when personal character is free from environmental control; when actions are guided by personal convictions and talents. From beneath uncounted millions of different faces emerged common conscious traits and energies. The composite has been described as a "human spirit", but in fact may be our true mindset, our true conscious nature. From here came the roses of success, as though within an intact perfect self throbs the pulse of humanity. But the pacemaker gene could not have been inherited from the predator-prey temporal world,— which in fact is an opposition.

That a person can become free from an oppressive mentality; that the manner defies physical understanding or instruction; that personal consciousness defies scientific explanation; that the actual character trait, and ability to become free is unlike anything physical; that activity from within personal character, or the individualist is authentic and spontaneous; that ideals as equality, freedom or truth exist only within personal consciousness; suggest human consciousness is quite different than we imagine; and so is God!

With the consideration of "self-evident" ideals as behavioral truths, and the formation of a government as our "self-defense" mechanism: the world essentially moved from physical, to a much deeper SELF-CONTROL!

For several reasons it seemed I could assume this transition to hold a more complex explanation than those explained in biological evolutional theories. Foremost, the direction is an opposition to survival of the most fit through physical prowess, or power. The believers in justice endured despite annihilation attempts by the more powerful Roman Empire, Catholic Church, Saracen invasion of Europe, British Empire or Nazi Regime. An inner conscious strength prevailed against superior intellectual strategy or physical power throughout all the major determining battles.

That everything in the human mind has a real source; that we only copy and utilize forms and principles already in existence; that perception seems the primary function or purpose of an integrated physical anatomy; that in addition to physical perceptions, we share common ideals as truth or freedom; that these common ideals have no physical characteristics, but seem pure unlimited conscious energies; that these ideals were realized and gained support as the word of Jesus spread across the globe; that after America gave freedom to these conscious ideals, or natural social conscience, we moved toward behavioral compatibility; that this common bond unified us, restored, or fit us into the whole picture where each division in nature expresses one behavior; that our one behavior is entirely authentic, spontaneous and free, is expressed in diverse manners,—defies written rules, is sensed only as an entity called 'fairness'; that this one behavior happened because of a personal ability to become free from an environmental mind; that unlike the case of ecosystems which contribute to the whole of the physical environment, humanity has no purpose; that the preferred, or ideal behavior of humanity is a distinct contrast to the natural predator-prey activity of other animals; that a superior brain capacity should make humanity simply a greater predator, but instead followed ideals as love and peace, and uses intellectual ability to prevent and protect from natural predatory events; that the acquisition of knowledge, or environmental truths does not seem relative to eons of cerebral, or physical evolution, but to a conscious attitude change, or self-maturation through prayer; that when America released this self-potential, an acceleration of progress ensued like no other period in history; that self-potential moved us from a mythical and synthetic reality created by the physical mind, to the REAL world; that as we prayed, environmental knowledge was acquired, and used to prevent, and protect from natural pathology and catastrophe; that the knowledge also moved us toward improved communication; toward cohesion of self, formerly separated by conditions of time, place and person; and most of all that where other divisions of nature are programmed with a uniform behavior, in humanity the uniformity exists only within personal consciousness as a free flowing formless indefinable energy; that our natural social conscience is composed of pure conscious energies called ideals; which existed separate of personal awareness, until religious coercion to introspection through a perspective introduced by Jesus, evoked what seems a natural conformity, which leads not to uniform behavior, but a compatible DIVERSITY and creativity!

All suggesting the physical line of demarcation for human perception is not real. This physical line encapsulates humanity in a synthetic reality, and a person in a mind formed by that reality. Physicists have demonstrated energy 'just is', came from nothing. So in likeness to the concept of a flat world, the entire image of physical separation and search for answers out there could be wrong. Truth most likely is not distant, just not perceived because of the way we think,—the way we apply perspectives of time, distance and form to thought.

Underneath the predatory appearance of natural movement, we found a homeostatic mechanism of earth and body. This could suggest original potential for everlasting life. As each person enters an already existent knowledge, so could have humanity. The physical world is essentially a life-support machine. We reveal knowledge of how it works. Planet earth is composed of specific integrated mechanisms. This fact tends to support consideration of a Creator. Like all machines, the physical world could have been introduced to an already existent conscious world by a Creator. The Biblical explanation that the heavens and earth preceded man coincides with scientific theories, as does our 'earthy' composition. That we are able to extract knowledge of how the machine works could suggest conscious connection to that Creator; or could simply be an intellectual adaptive mechanism.

Where our body resembles other animals, and our mind holds physical reflections, our self, our invisible person may be far more. Within each person exists a common world called the American Dream! American social arrangement in likeness to all living things, where energy flows from the inside-out, moved us rapidly toward truths and compatibility. Like each cell in the body contributes to the welfare of the whole, so may be the nature of reality. A person reveals a truth; the thought is shared; thus, we abandon myths and tediously find our reality. As the body is dependent on each cell; reality seems dependent on each person's mental capacity, or conscious contribution. Truths entered our world from the inside-out! As though the real world existed, and probably still exists in millions of conscious pieces. We used these contributions of truth, or scientific principles to design technology to improve communication. Our means to better access more knowledge! God may not have been a silent partner during our ascent!

It became my opinion that through a focus on religious teaching and prayer, we somehow reached a better personal identity, or understanding of SELF, which released a greater conscious depth potential. Consideration of current social changes strengthened that idea. With prayer removed from public education, we seem to lose spontaneity of ideas, and many resume more narrow and shallow lifestyles. With money as the goal, and scientific authority in control; we may have disconnected from our energy source, lost sight of our guide. The image of a man, who walked around the countryside, helped people in miraculous ways and always treated people fairly, dims.

We are now presented with exact physical laws, structured analysis and mathematical formulas. Children seem to have become dependent on precise instruction, on the computer; and become swept into the mind of their friends. Intuition may have been buried under facts. Work assignments came down from above, from a distant central authority. Deluded and distanced from truth, and carefully programmed; we comply.

Then the thought entered my mind that humanity really does nothing original. Either copies perceptions delivered by the physical senses, or abstract conscious perceptions. Acquired information is used to create, but within limitations of a knowledge that already exists. Still, there has been an authenticity in personal behavior and personal relationships. There seem to be conscious distinctions between humanity and other animals, most especially surrounding the existence and nature of our common ideals. Also in the manner we don't have to adapt, or behave in a predator-prey; manner but can make our own reality. Success for an individual, and humanity seems to surround our ability to share thought, with progressive ideation and innovations flowing from those with deep personal convictions. Realization of truths, creativity and compatibility seem related not to cerebral mechanics alone, but to certain personal character strengths. All seems to suggest somewhere in the nature of personal consciousness exists the key to identity. It became curious to me that we search for physical evidence when throughout all the eras, it has been prayer, a personal conscious experience that has provided the answer for the individual.

Despite acquisition of the basic knowledge of human anatomy, the mind and individual behavior remains largely an enigma. Where physical traits are known to be genetic inheritances, so could memories be. There is no scientific formula to describe the composition of thought! The basic human behavioral problem, the cause of negative emotional responses and conflict, seems to be for one to desire power over another. Periodically ideation to control the world emerges. Could this ideation be a vestigial memory? In any way relative to the Biblical story of 'the fall', or the 'devil'? Everything in the human mind has a real source, and we copy what we see. Obviously there is a negative, a predatory motion that overpowers and brings things to an end in the physical environment. This would be the more tangible entity we copy. But where did this predatory motion come from? It conflicts with the intrinsic homeostatic arrangement of body and environment; and a human conscious desire for love and everlasting life. If this negative motion is part of our original environment; and if we were merely products of biological ascension; our superior brain should intrinsically enable us as predators. Instead we find predation emotionally uncomfortable. I believe an individual can either be taught compatible behavior, or express a real live authentic inherent 'goodness'. Is it the same case with bad behavior? Is this entirely acquired due to individual circumstance, or can an individual be inherently bad? Some people do express an especially strong desire to overpower and cause harm. Overall direction would support that good or bad behavior can be determined by an individual circumstance as to physiology, including perhaps a genetic memory transfer, combined with environmental conditions. But that within each mind so formed exists an intact perfect person, which is an equal possession and therefore holds an inherent goodness, or means to compatibility. It seems like the process of self-awareness is the source of natural goodness. A person can become free from a behavior causing unhappiness. The dominant choice of the individual, and humanity has been to escape from predator-prey behavior in its entirety. Unlike other animals we have proven the ability to neither became a predator,—or the prey.

Everything in the human mind has a real source. Unless a world of love and peace were in existence, where would this idea come from? A basic principle is that an organism be compatible with its environment. That predatory behavior is incompatible, and love is compatible seems to suggest that mankind emerged from a conscious world far different from the motion in this physical environment. That the direction away from predation is relative to character strengths gained through prayer to a God of LOVE; that during this time we massed knowledge to protect and prevent harm from predatory natural events as illness, hurricanes or floods; and that we moved toward compatibility of environment and people; all seemed to strengthen the idea of human relationship to a greater conscious existence; and one with greater strength than the evil, or harmful motions in our world. Predatory behavior is futile! Every predator eventually encounters a greater predator. Predation is the cause of endings!

It then occurred to me that another marked difference emerged after God was dismissed from public instruction and communication. Historic documents and records clearly reflect credence in God and understanding of ideals as equality, truth or personal worth by the leaders who guided America to greatness. These ideals were considered "self-evident" Rights. This seems to be exactly what they are. Pure conscious entities found within each invisible person, or 'self'. "Endowed by their Creator with certain unalienable Rights." These considered inherent rights are ethereal ideas with no organic attributes. The ideals have been enduring conscious needs of social exchange throughout all the eras. Our constitution is an open door to creation of a social reality where satisfaction of those common ideals could be possible.

It became my contention that when America began, it was designed with intent for satisfaction of common social needs,—which were considered rights determined by nature and nature's God. As the place these rights can be found is deep within each person, or SELF,—for an eventual collective SELF-REALIZATION. However, mankind has perpetuated a primitive mentality formed by the appearance of environmental activity in the animal world. Perpetuates what appeared to be a hierarchy system determined by competition for material gain through physical power control. This is the image that controlled, and continues to control social affairs on an individual, and international level. A power control system is embedded deep in the governing mind, where a belief coercion is necessary continues to this day. Therefore, the believers in justice, or human rights; from Christ throughout all eras, including early America, were not readily accepted. Human rights activists endured, and still endure much hardship. Like all truths, time was necessary before realization. The major protests against oppression were always eventually victorious, and directed our course. Again this happened when God and prayer was associated with the ideals. The effects were all of a conscious nature, and directed toward common welfare.

Equality was introduced in areas relative to common needs. For example: happiness is dependent on the nature of our social environment; voting rights were extended. We all arrive with a wide-open consciousness; public education was started. Compassion and equality radiated from the health care professions. We all desire well-being, but will suffer illness. Government agencies were created to encourage business integrity, and protect consumers. Truth mattered. The accused are to be assumed innocent until truth could be discerned. Peace was valued. Aggression begets aggression. America was only to wage war in self-defense. Freedom was from oppression, or harm by another person or group.

All these social changes seem reflections of a common inner vision. It seems almost as though something was guiding us toward 'heaven on earth'. It could be that increased episodes of personal connection to God through prayer evoked a personal identity; a self-awareness, that through a sort of conscious cohesion, was moving the social world toward personal satisfaction. Still, all remained within the control of an outer restrictive barrier, the still oppressive nature of the human establishment. Then, in the sixties a movement was started by the coming generation to demand love and peace. Even though by this time the outer barrier was stretched thin, it had the stronghold. The ideal mind exists within the heart of the people; the oppressive mind in governing authority, or 'the establishment'. These minds are an opposition to each other, but in physical conflicts, or protests; the ideal mind could not be annihilated. Kept expanding, stretching the outer barrier thin like the air in a balloon. Just when it seemed ready to burst, the strength of the current diminished.

Revered leaders, idealists were assassinated. The media focused, and projected the 'bad' activities related to the movement. Even the religious establishment denounced this 'love and peace' movement. The secular establishment moved minds back to their world. To which people soon adapted, the ideal mind began to fade. Vision became shallow. People obeyed rules to get things. Willingly gave up their freedom, soon were plugged into an emerging social machine. Believed what they were told. Became indebted to the aristocratic factions that have always ruled mankind. Wallowing in comfort, told those with suspicions all this was a lie, to 'get real'!

Scientific education directed vision back to the physical world strengthening the illusion, and the outer restrictive barrier to personal growth. The only difference between now and pre-America seems to be in depth perception. Then, social reality was based on appearance of objects; where now seems a simulation of the mechanics, or actual governing physical principles. The physical world follows natural laws, and with our mind now attached to this view, we became flooded with rules and regulations. There is no freedom in any physical structure, all parts are inter-related. The freedom extended in America existed within personal consciousness, within thought. It was of a personal nature; a personal freedom from an acquired oppressive mentality. Likewise there is no physical equality. A man and woman are not equal in body or mind. No two people are equal, not even identical twins. Equality exists only within personal consciousness, where each is in essence only a receiver of perceptions. Thought moves the body. When we believed in everlasting life, we prolonged life; when we believed in equal personal worth, we started public services—and so on. Where educational opportunity expanded, means toward personal character realization was not included. America provided an opportunity to bring a social environment into existence compatible with what seems an inherent human conscience.

The 'soul' of America is not visible, but a conscious sense of fairness; the 'human spirit' is not visible, but is a pure conscious energy surrounding this sense of fairness; and the source of American success, what moved the social world toward compatibility with this invisible sense of fairness—is not visible,—flowed from personal character strengths; from those who had self-awareness,—knew just who they were!

The overall view of our course seems to show two basic changes. Increased episodes of self-awareness, and social freedom of this personal inner vision. Once considered natural requirements, this energy from within brought forth spontaneous ideas seemingly capable of unlimited actualities. We must wonder was academia deluded? Smothered in detail and facts, did they fail to notice the difference between personal consciousness, and the physical world? Is the decline of our standing as a nation in matters of morality, intellectual achievement and prosperity due to failure of academia to consider personal consciousness in its entirety? Of utmost interest to me, was the failure of the sixties movements. Could it have been because for the first time the screams for justice were dissociated from God?

My Dilemma

I don't get it! I just don't get it! I believe the American Constitution was formed in accordance with conscious laws predetermined by "Nature and Nature's God." Laws expressed in words about things not visible to the eyes, not detectable by any of the five senses.

Through prayer our ancestors came together in thought. Promoted awareness of a natural social conscience, a spirit that is ours. When the American Liberty Bell rang, it was this spirit buried deep in thought that gained freedom. It can be defined as a belief in equality, truth, freedom, peace, compassion, personal ability and everlasting life. Identity with this conscience is a personal conscious experience; it can't be defined in any other way. This identity, or inherent common expectations of social exchange formed the American road toward justice, or happiness.

Ascension of humanity seems an entity separate from physical evolution. Consciousness is the living growing thing! Like the little child is unaware of a parent's reality; humanity was unaware of physical and behavioral truths that always existed. Progress in essence seems a conscious maturation. An awareness of the

REAL world. Freedom from an erroneous mind! The human course was not determined by intellectual or military supremacy. Not by more powerful religious or social government establishments. Not by any change in the anatomy or physiology of our brain. The evolutionary events relative to progress occurred within our mind. Progress is made possible because a REAL world, a truth exists; which we have a capacity to realize. Attitude changes account for our rise! The strength that guided us to victory in all major conflict radiated from a growing awareness of common social needs.

The American colonists had no blueprint to follow. Perhaps guided by "the lamp that shines from above," they entered that abyss we call the future. The WAY, inaudible to the ear. Perhaps broadcast on a higher frequency! With the Bible as the primary textbook. And how to become a better person the basic education. We began to soar toward unlimited actualities!

America is more than a geographic location. It is a still unfulfilled dream that has lived in the heart of humanity throughout all the eras. The dream could have been brought forth through effort of all religious instruction toward personal prayer. This directed vision away from earth's predatory appearance, to a place within each person. I just don't get it! We dig for archeological findings to find solution for existence. But the answer instead seems buried deep in thought!

The body seems an automatic copy machine. Evident in little children imitating siblings and parents. In the existence of local languages, accents, cultural and occupational styles. This mechanical mind formed by the appearance of activity and objects in our environment is limited. Relative to a specific point in time, place and individual perceptive physiology. The shape of planet earth to the immediate physical view is flat. It is not!

Scientific truths are not acquired, or realized separate from personal effort. Truths are not automatic mental acquisitions. Not part of the images delivered by the five senses and body mechanics. Scientific and behavioral principles are buried under appearance. And realized deep in thought! We can't see the basic elements, protoplasm, anatomy and physiology or the mechanics of pathology at a glance. We certainly can't see a message carried by the central nervous system. So is the person buried under the body! We can't see the person, but only the body!

Personal consciousness, or thought itself seems an entity separate from any physical substance. There is no scientific formula to describe the composition of thought. Truths entered our world from within personal thought. Always meeting ridicule and resistance from academic, religious, prestigious social or government establishments. But we do have a desire for, and a capacity to realize truth. Thought is shared. Truth eventually comprehended, and becomes known. Myths are abandoned. It is our means of growth, of maturation. Made possible because a knowledge,—a REAL world exists beyond our immediate physical awareness. Which we have the capacity to perceive.

When we look at someone, we see only the body. Not the person. It is the person we grow to love and respect. No matter what shape the body is in! A person is not a physical object. A person is an invisible thought! Perhaps so is the invisible God in which uncounted millions, and most especially the American founders placed credence! American rights are not linear, but protect the person. Not metaphysical explanations, religious definitions or scientific truths, but personal prayer provided personal identity and satisfaction. There may be an actual conscious connection. We copy images. What better image to inspire connection than the person, the strength of a loving father? What better inspired progress than the image of the behavior of Jesus, the sense of fairness, which became the ideals of American government? In God we trust was a sound investment, even before it radiated from our currency. Herein may be philosophic solution!

Before America, governing methods were oppressive, in likeness to the predatory physical motion. Such systems are futile. It is a negative motion. Greater powers as earthquakes, volcanic eruptions, tornadoes, fires or floods destroy. The same with people. When one tries to have power over the other, destruction or death can be the effect. In the animal world eventually every predator succumbs to a greater predator. As did nations who copy this style. Perhaps, explaining the rise and fall of human regimes! The only positive motion in our world flowed with human ideals. It could be the 'power of prayer' was very real. All indications are that the only reason for our current decline is reversion to 'outside' instruction; to separation from the true image of the American Dream; a state of personal satisfaction, of justice.

Oppressive social systems endured until people reached the brink of their endurance. Colonial American fervor suggests existence of burning desires for SELF-expression. The American Declaration of Independence clearly expresses recognition that tyranny conflicts with certain unalienable, or God given rights. Although the concept of democracy may trace to ancient Athens, the difference in early America may have been prevalence of the belief justice is dependent on satisfaction of those ethereal rights; on the strength of the human spirit. America was instrumental in enforcing personal responsibility to adhere to those rights. The government was given to this natural morality, or 'common sense' of the people; as was the justice system. God was the common denominator. The Bible still remains in the courtroom as a means to encourage truth. Freedom was from power control by any human establishment. Allowing an individual to have personal proximity to God.

Man is projected as being the highest product of an evolutionary chain. But there is also the scientific fact that energy once used is never of the same quality. Religion and science seem to agree that something went wrong in the beginning. There is no longer the perfect gas; the perfect oak tree; the perfect human. I don't get it! I just don't get it!! Would it not be more likely the animals lower on the food chain were once humans? Jainism may hold wisdom in the belief one should never harm a living thing. It could be our ancestor!

Analogy of human to other animal life seems worthy of consideration. Similarity seems only in the body machine,—in anatomy and physiology. There are human peculiarities in biological behavior. A human non-compliance to some basic biological principles can be recognized. That an organism be compatible with its environment is vital. But ecologists sound the alarm. Proclaim mankind is destroying the machine,—his own natural habitat, on which survival depends. An animal instinctively knows its environment and demonstrates uniform behavior within its realm. Humanity tediously acquires environmental knowledge. May still have barely penetrated the surface of the real world. The human doesn't even know its nutrition or exercise necessities. With resultant mass obesity and pathology.

It seems somewhat a paradox that humanity is given supremacy in a biological chain; when unlike other organisms, who contribute harmoniously to the overall environment; humanity exists without any identifiable purpose. Other than maybe if there is a devil, or evil entity trying to destroy the creation, as the Christian religion preaches. It has always been difficult for me to even consider such a notion. To me it seems most likely a projection of the immature and oppressive mentality of the ancient Biblical writers; as well as early religious hierarchy, who chose what to include. Jesus too, could have just used it as means to communicate right behavior to the mind of His era. Some event indefinable to our limited minds must have happened though. The extrinsic predatory motion that brings things to an end really does not fit into the big picture. Why would a physical body and environment with an intrinsic arrangement to provide continuous existence; and what is considered the highest species desire everlasting life; find themselves in a contrary place? Why would this highest species not be guided by the intrinsic desire for love and everlasting life? Where did this negative motion to which our minds have attached, and direct us toward a potential for ultimate destruction through nuclear warfare come from? We definitely have a conscious defect, a perceptual disorder. Despite intellectual superiority, humans arrive ignorant of basic talent, behavior and adaptive mechanisms. Where organisms lower on the hierarchy scale arrive equipped by nature to assume a role; the human must be carefully taught. Often because of social conditions, many never express a particular talent. And those who do must practice, practice, practice!

The predator-prey behavior expressed by humanity is also a curiosity. In other animals it is among different species. One species is a predator, another is prey. Where in humans, predator-prey activity exists within the human species itself, by individuals and groups. While at the same time the human species suggests a common aversion to this behavior in its entirety. The 'hero' is never a predator, and is seemingly invincible,—does not fall prey! Protects others from predators. The American Constitution is designed to protect people from oppression,—or the master-slave,—predator-prey mentality. In contrast to the visible biological motion, American laws are founded on an inner conscious vision,—do not allow predatory behavior. Intent was to eradicate tyranny. By government, or any individual, or institution during personal social exchange; or by American representatives in foreign affairs. Antipathy to predator-prey activity is suggested by all social reform. That compatible behavior is contrary to other biological motion seems a human distinction!

Where in other biological life, genetic inheritance determines purpose and behavior. And principles of the theory of evolution, as natural selection, adaptation and survival of the most fit determine direction. With humanity, religion seems the determinate factor. Worship of the supernatural can be traced to cave dwellings. Religious beliefs were cornerstones of community laws. Judaic-Christian principles were the basic contributory elements to the behavior and development of western civilization. Could this persistent notion of greater existence not be some sort of vestigial memory? Most especially as it always existed, and continues to exist worldwide, with conflict only being in physical interpretation. Truths reach common agreement; variable physical minds conflict. Could this not suggest the belief in God is the truth, and what is not real is the mind formed by the outside; be it from physical appearance, or opinion of other people? Should this not be of concern as contributions of scientific truths to the establishment, seem to have empowered this ruling materialistic mind?

It almost seems like the most basic human problem could be that the individual, and humanity is controlled by a mentality other than its own. All the prolific and compatible elements in our world seem to exist on the inside. Overshadowed by a mind that is inaccurate. It could be an everlasting world is right in our midst, but occult because our thought is formed through a physical perspective. This could be the reason for the sense of isolation from the whole of reality. There are those who through meditation sense a sort of freedom from physical boundaries, a oneness that can't be explained in material terms. It seems like all conscious awareness is automatically converted to material thought, and communicated through a vocabulary based on physical entities. This may be best exemplified by early religious rituals and animal sacrifices; by the concept of anthropomorphism itself; the many secular myths, most especially the reality in which the world was flat. That physical conversion would be a natural mechanism makes sense, but the inaccuracy and incompatibility of the view so formed does not. We may consider inaccuracy relative to a primitive brain and mind, but that too may stem from our seemingly fixed perspective based on appearance. It does not explain reason for incompatibility, which seems relative to the nature of the invisible person, or SELF. The search for truth; the truths; and realization of the truths all relates to the nature of personal consciousness. Again making the human SELF seem something different from the acquired, or physical mind. Where we abandoned some erroneous physical views, it seems we should end this limited mode of thinking in its entirety.

We can make an analogy of the conscious development in the child, to that of humanity. A child in considering just one new word expresses an imagination that opens a whole new world for them. The same with humanity. A scientist becomes aware of a physical principle, and humanity moves into a whole new reality. In both cases this flows from the inside, and is inhibited by fitting the idea into the prevailing overall mentality. It could be if we just stop believing what the outside tells us we are, a world would open for us beyond anybody's present ability to begin to comprehend. Our common sense of lack could be related to the way we think,—to not being true to ourselves. The materialistic mind has always ruled, and has been incompatible with inherent conscious needs. Instead we have been conditioned to support the greater physical strength, the establishment; not the person.

This is evident in all areas. Even the philanthropist will give to an organization, rather than to individuals. In my opinion every judge representing the ideation in our constitution should decide from the heart, from the inner conscious sense of truth. This ability is inhibited in each individual through coercive adaptation to the materialistic mind from birth. Foremost respect goes to an establishment over an individual; the best intellectual argument prevails; and only the wealthy can afford such defense. The energy of our ascent flowed out from within personal consciousness, moving the secular and religious establishment toward compatibility with common social needs. The two establishments have always fought each other for control of the people. Where the American Constitution should have ended the conflict by giving control to the people; it seems the people fell asleep at the wheel. This current fervor surrounding separation of Church-State most likely is just a return of the age-old conflict. There is a strong possibility this time people are being deluded by the 'state', the secular establishment, who desires to again control them. Despite an oppressive structure, the strong emotional attachment of people to religion, may be relative to a need for natural conscious connection to God; just misinterpreted; again because of age-old conditioning toward dependency on the establishment. Today, more than ever, people are being trained to comply, being engulfed by the establishment. Fewer express authenticity, their own mind. That this is despite academic and psychological direction to 'be yourself' could suggest more than intelligence is necessary. The personal freedoms from erroneous minds through deeper reasoning ability that released character strengths may be relative to meditation, to the God connection of our predecessors. Does the fact love is our primary conscious need; and has been the motivator of humanity; not suggest a human to be more than a physical creature? Is not the fact that the image of God moved from a greater predator, to a loving father of significance? Is it wise to abandon this idea that absorbed so many people, and brought great strength and success to a nation? Have we overlooked the ethereal nature of American ideology? Words as freedom, peace, equality, truth, love or justice have no earthy identity. In fact, are they not an opposition to visible physical activity?

To reiterate; human social establishments seem reflections, or copies of environmental appearance. Hierarchy systems, where the most powerful wear the diadem. Truths, or natural principles are not physical sensory acquisitions. But realized deep in thought! We discovered and began rudimentary development and utilization of deeper mental resources. Penetration of our mind was a precedent to the realization of truths. Then we began to realize many perceptions and concepts on environmental structure and activity were illusions.

We now know that energy in all living things flows from the INSIDE-OUT! A simple gametic union develops into a complex human. Where each cell has a purpose. Contributes harmoniously to form an organ. Uniting in a system. Working collectively as a machine. Every organism displays a similar mechanism. Including our entire physical environment, mother earth. Where each member blends into an eco-system. Acting collectively to form what seems an overall 'LIFE-SUPPORT' machine!

The theory of evolution suggests all life can be traced to a single cell in the ocean. Every organism, or bodily part develops in similar fashion. Except the human mind! Traditionally formed from the OUTSIDE-IN! By environmental perceptions, opinions of others;—family, social, political, or religious laws. As though the person;—the SELF, or anatomic holder of these perceptions were dormant. Buried under a synthetic mind formed merely through extraneous body mechanics. Was it not religious teachings surrounding compassion; retreats from the physical world for personal prayer and contemplation that contributed to release of this inner self,—or perhaps the REAL human mind?

To reflect on our course, it may become evident where we tend to favor an establishment of body, or theory; over an individual act, or opinion; and authority, over common sense; the 'outside' over the inside; it is the 'outside' mind that has proven incorrect, and it is the 'inside' that moves it toward truth and compatibility. Could it not be considered the 'outside' mind is a reflection of environmental appearance and activity? A mind acquired from appearance, or an 'outside' world through our physical senses? An 'inner consciousness' has proven this mind of physiological adaptation to hold many errors, especially in regard to the master-slave affair, and oppressive behavior. We can see as we find truths, we become free from this 'outer' restrictive mentality. I believe Jesus suggested that 'the truth would set us free'. Social focus on the teachings of Buddha, Jesus and Mohammed and personal meditation preceded, and accompanied us on our rapid ascent. On what may have been a freedom flight, an escape from control by a mind that is wrong. We may have dismissed our guides before even recognizing the road we traveled, let alone sight of our destination. Personal meditation was a way of life. Abandonment of this practice may have interrupted our journey. We may have once more been deceived by appearance. Our journey was not linear, but was bringing us together at a place somewhere deep within personal thought. Now we seem to have been removed from this place, and once more become dependent on 'outside' human authority. It is possible this could again immobilize us. Of concern is the fact the deeper message of Biblical passages no longer seems to be perceived. Support for evidence the Bible does, or does not project the word of God is all based on literal interpretation. The positive effect of the Bible and Golden Rule seems relative to personal character growth. In actuality moved thought away from words about physical things. Where it was when individuals adhered to, and social laws moved toward compliance with the unspoken Golden Rule, or understood the words we call 'human ideals' that a just society seemed within range; the art of life seems to dwindle, and we instead interpret the written word in an instruction or contract as truth. Our vocabulary has primitive roots, flows from a mentality limited to physical appearance. American founders proved there is more to human consciousness. That truths flow from what is abstract!

The Bible and a Golden Rule were the navigators of western civilization. Both in essence penetrate the 'outer' mind, reach the 'self', emit an unspoken language, as do the writings of our founders. The knowledge within 'self' never changes. Truths and personal deeper reasoning potential always existed, just separate from our awareness. There is a conscious sense of another person's character that accompanies social exchange. This 'inner' person is what stays with us, what matters. There is an abstract language in social exchange that makes life an art. Mastering this art seems what moved us toward compatibility; and the deeper reasoning ability toward truths. Should it continue it seems possible we may find we have no boundary, and neither does our world. If not from the person our ancestors called God, where then did this 'inner person', and this common 'inner consciousness' come from?

Our consciousness may be of an unlimited nature, just remains encapsulated in an outer physical perspective. The mind that is formed from the outside-in holds an image of things that appear to begin and end, and come from something else. Our mind is formed by images. These physical images move our thought to suspect we have a beginning, and to look for it 'out there'. Our course clearly shows images form our mind, some are concrete, others abstract. At this point of what is called progress it is possible to see awareness of environmental truths flowed out from within personal consciousness. In essence from someone who cleared a personal abstract idea, as Pasteur, the Wright brothers, Thomas Edison, Einstein and so on. We also hold abstract behavioral ideals as equality, freedom, compassion and personal worth and allowance for these beliefs to flow from the inside-out seems what led America to prosperity. Throughout all the eras humanity has held an abstract image of God and everlasting life. And nothing has mattered more, had a greater emotional impact. Jesus was low on the social hierarchy scale; His message flowed from the inside out; from an earthy nobody in Jerusalem out across the globe. The message He gave was for each person to develop through personal prayer to God; in essence form a mind from the inside-out. The quantum theory suggests the physical world to be an illusion; there is no separation; all is inter-related. Buddhist meditation allows a personal escape from the physical mind to sense oneness with our world. Like our inner consciousness made outer changes, so could God have brought us into existence, a reality so unlike ours based on physical appearance, it becomes indescribable. Heaven most likely is not 'out there'; not some distant place; to get there we may just have to change the way we think!

Adaptation to the reality formed by environmental perceptions proved incompatible. The SELF, harboring emotional needs for entities as equality, peace, love truth and freedom. An opposition to the master-slave, or predator-prey mentality. There can be no equality or freedom when one has power over another. Negative emotions are inevitable.

Inadvertently natural psychological defense mechanisms developed. Perhaps to protect the SELF. Power control in actuality is the root of unhappiness. The culminate effect of inability to satisfy emotional needs,—most especially love, becomes a neurosis. A human malady. Common to all. Just varying in degree.

A person, or the part of mental anatomy called SELF is the receiver, filter and response center for perceptions. So, it would seem SELF-CONTROL is a decree of nature. Instead, the person can be developed and controlled by the perceptions. This human outside-in mental development seems an anomaly to basic overall biological structure. As though humanity sustained some psychological trauma. Or SELF is a vestigial remnant of a prior different,—a compatible reality! Eras of character development through prayer seemed to bring forth SELF-AWARENESS. After freedom for self-development was allowed by America,— we came to life!

The New World was more than a place. It was an idea. One that followed a natural grain. Dimensions were reduced as people bonded through 'the spirit'. Their success should dismiss consideration of this 'spirit' to be mystical, and instead recognize it as our source of strength,—our true mindset, an intrinsic will of the people. Resistance to power control is inherent. The epitome of an ideal democracy would seem a world where each person is co-equal in power. To reach this destination would demand compliance with ONE ideology, or 'spirit' of harmonious inter-relationship. Directions to this place called equality already exist deep within personal thought.

I don't get it! I just don't get it! To contemplate on the human course with advantage of the scientific and historical knowledge of this era; combined with the effect an attempt to dissociate the concept of personal worth and love from its relativity to God, has had on social circumstances should strengthen, or add validity to the unspoken message of all major religions,—most especially Christianity. Instead we again allow the environment to control us; we obey and copy;—resume a masquerade. It could have been personal introspection through religious teachings and meditation that promoted attitude changes. Evoked awareness of pure conscious social ideals. After America formed a government in likeness to natural structure, it opened a door for this dream to materialize. This conscious energy could be our true SELF. Unlike other animals with uniform behavior, humanity through this mind expressed a compatible diversity. We now seem guided toward a robotic conformity. Oblivious to an occult suggestion that an intact PERFECT SELF may have been guiding us to a perfect world!

The Masquerade

Worship of supernatural powers seems a distinctly human peculiarity. Other animals seem endowed by physical nature with environmental knowledge, and survival mechanisms. But somehow in the transition from ape, humanity seems to have lost identity. You really don't have to know where you are, to be there! And this ludicrous fact remains the human predicament.

Our primitive ancestors really did not know what they were, or where they were. And we still don't. Maybe because we perpetuate the basic reality they formed in their extremely immature state. This could even explain why our research is directed on the origin and development of the human body. Be the reason we are so absorbed with finding evidence to verify physical ascension. The early human mind would have been little more than a product of the body; of images delivered to an isolated person through the physical senses. The mind was formed by things that are 'out there'. This perception continues to be the root of our thought process. We continue to look for answers 'out there'. These primitive images were also of what appeared to be a natural hierarchy arrangement, determined by physical power. We remain subservient to authority figures, and seem to depend on their guidance. This too could be a lingering primitive idea. We still expect some authority figure out there to supply us with the answers we search for. To consider the advent, and course of human civilization; rather suggests what we should be examining is not our body, but our thought. Answer to the origin of our life may not be found in our bones and brains; but within the nature of our consciousness. Because not our animated body; but consciousness is the life of the body; the life of our world. That 'all comes down from above' is an illusion; the energy of our ascent flowed like in all living things, from the 'inside-out'; from within personal consciousness.

Quantum mechanics demonstrates the appearance of isolated forms is inaccurate. Everything is interrelated. Biologists describe ascension of organisms; but ecologists warn of descent of the natural environment. There is the problem of entropy, and energy once used is never of the same quality. Any interference with nature holds an unpredictable effect, some of which are undesirable. Scientists also say everything has descended from perfection. There is no longer the perfect gas, oak tree or human. It is said only a very small portion of human brain potential is utilized. We have an intrinsic homeostatic mechanism of body and environment; but contrasting intermittent outer motions that overpower the normal state, as disease, winds, floods or earthquakes; and tend to bring things to an end. We believed the objective world to be truth, but Einstein said reality is an illusion. Indications are there was an original formation, or ascension; which at some point experienced a catastrophic change. The outer negative motion could not be original, as it is an opposition to the intrinsic arrangement for continuous existence. This physical change would alter human physical sensory perception, as now both the body and environmental machine are in essence defective. Suggesting we should sever any ties to primitive human thought.

THE LONG OVERDUE LETTER

The outer forms and negative motion was the only thing visible to an isolated primitive eye. The human body not only automatically delivers perceptions, but also tends to copy environmental actions. This is evident in a child copying parents; or an adult entering an unfamiliar setting will copy the actions of others. Of course it is also evident in the similar behaviors of variable cultures and groups. We can see a simulation of the animal predator-prey behavior, in the human master-slave affair. This is still very much in existence, just more sophisticated, and holds less brutality. It should be obvious by now this is a masquerade. Humans make lousy masters, as social conditions remain incompatible, and they have not been the contributors toward progress; in fact have inhibited individual creativity and truths. To be enslaved is contrary to an inherent human nature, which craves freedom. This practice has not only caused much grief, but also inhibited the release of talent for the welfare of the whole. Retention of this primitive view is probably our greatest mistake. The system tends to paralyze, and is the root of overall unhappiness. We are all dependent on each other, and all have a talent. For all to become teachers and students would be a far more natural arrangement.

We can see the fallacy in all of the basic premises on which our reality is based. To continue with this primitive mind frame is insanity. This is the mindset of the human establishment, and it did not move forward with American progress; but kept its feet planted firmly on the ground. No establishment within adopted the new system of leadership. Inner rulers were not swayed by the respect for personal worth, and the mindset of inherent social ideals that form the soul of our Constitution. Still, the new governing mind did put some restraint on oppressive old world leadership style, allowing energy to flow out from the heart of the people. The success brought forth should verify the colonial founders were correct in their premise the mindset called 'human ideals' is our true natural endowment; our real mind. Instead of following the natural course, old world establishments, including religions incorporated, and contrary to our constitution monopolized, and begin to control our government. Where the ideal mindset on which our country is based, was moving us toward what seemed would be unlimited growth, it again is being restrained. We follow because we never escaped the mind formed by things, or the need for subservience to something 'out there'. Another primitive root is the 'begin and end' mentality range. The mind is of forms; and forms appear to begin and end. Thought moves the body. As long as this mindset rules, we will follow the course of the things from which it is derived. We will continue to bring things into existence that will be temporary, as in the case of nations, will 'rise and fall'.

The early human saw events like the larger animal devour the weaker, or the volcano erupt and cause devastation. Thus, a foundation formed with an implication personal survival is dependent on degree of physical power. Despite the evidence today that our strength came from within personal character; we retain that primitive mentality. We continue the illusive reality based on competition for intellectual and physical superiority. The natural mechanism would surround personal growth; deliver a satisfaction of personal achievement. Instead we attach social reward in a manner that the effect is to gain power, over another. Until we escape respect for physical power, there will always be harmful activity. To overpower another always requires the use of force. Most especially we need to abandon the idea that police 'force' is the way to establish justice. When one person overpowers another, it is always an injustice. To overpower inhibits satisfaction of inherent social needs as equality, freedom, or compassion; so always is an injustice. There is but one source of conflict, and that is injustice. War is the most horrendous human activity arising from these primitive mental roots; this respect for physical power.

We may not know where we came from, but one thing is certain. The cave is definitely not where we where we were meant to be. We have proven intellectual capacity to unravel earth's structure and find a more compatible place. What seems to go unrecognized is our escape has not been through military supremacy, or linear direction; but guided by those who found disparity with the oppressive mindset, and followed personal convictions. Knowledge as to behavior and environmental truths was not distant, but in our midst the entire journey! We found the mind formed by eyesight was an illusion. The reflections delivered by the physical senses were incorrect. We discovered vision occurs within consciousness, within the invisible person, the Self; made a conscious transition, brought truths into view. This mindset from within moved us toward comfort and compatibility; is what made the difference.

We are physiologically adapted to earth. Our nose is the link to the universe. We anxiously await the newborn's first breathe. Earth is fondly considered our 'mother'. She is our life support machine. We love to see things grow! Much poetry surrounds our aesthetic connection to nature. Today the alarm sounds. She is in danger. Problems as diminishing natural resources, air pollution causing global warming are intensified. Ecologists consider human behavior the culprit. The children scream; beg the oppressors to stop hurting her. The rulers hold an ingrained quest for physical power; do not hear. The establishment that rules never matured; retains its primitive ideation.

Objects in the physical world appear to have a beginning and an end. Such was the sensory view to our primitive ancestors, and became the range of human thought passed on through the generations. Thus, we search for the beginning, and contemplate the end of existence. To consider the nature of the REAL physical world, which continues to hide under appearance, and is realized only within, through our entirely subjective conscious senses, and deeper reasoning; could show the beginning and ending mentality merely an illusion. Escape from this mind then would not only be possible; but should become a vital enterprise. Thought moves the body, and so there is not only the more obvious terminal destination for us; but somehow this negativity could have been inspired by an original consciousness of man, should the Bible story in Genesis hold any validity.

We now know that in actuality nothing entirely begins and ends, but only changes form. The theory of evolution describes truths of biological changes, as do physical sciences reveal the nature of conversions of matter. These truths are realized, or become visible within thought. A human body can only perceive what is already in existence. Physical principles always existed. Human conscious capacity for their realization always existed. As humanity was unaware of this conscious capacity, the truths, or physical principles that compose the REAL world were essentially non-existent. Thus humanity existed in, and expanded an unreal, or synthetic world acquired through an automatic linear sensory apparatus.

Philosophers tend to separate human reality, with one group supporting objectivism; the other subjectivism. It seems like objectivism is the case of human reality; but subjectivism is the case of true reality; to which human reality was incorporated. Human reality is not composed of pure physical substance; it is not entirely objective. Nor is it of an entirely conscious nature; it is not entirely subjective. The overall scheme of our world is a REAL, or objective; and IDEA, or subjective interchange. A REAL objective world appears in human thought. Every creation of humanity is a copy of an organic, or physical mechanism already in existence. All human mechanical inventions follow the already existent basic physical structure where separate parts are assigned a task, which harmoniously interrelate to form a unit, which contribute to form a system,—producing the whole. Objective and subjective is one entity. Existence of an object can only be determined by thought. A thought without an object becomes a void. The human body machine automatically takes the outside in. The images form a mind. A human body can only copy what already exists. So, to the human mind, there never was, and can never be a nothing. It is an impossible perception. Mind and object are necessary for composition of human reality.

Evidence to support the theory of our creation by a greater conscious existence may be found in the nature of this perceptive mechanism. Where it is possible to recognize cerebral activity, and physical energy responsible for the transmission, in likeness to technological imaging; there is no physical formula to describe the receiver,—or personal consciousness. The physical world is not only necessary to sustain the human body, but both are necessary to provide a reality; to enable us to see each other through the physical senses, our primary adaptive device. The 'person' in actuality seems a pure conscious entity, only an awareness of existence. Physical senses provide information about the body; not the person. Detection of personal character is an entirely personal conscious experience. The primary purpose of the human body seems to be to experience existence. All organs are necessary to support the brain, which transmits messages to and from personal consciousness. However, it seems unlikely personal consciousness is formed by the body because a person has no form, no physical substance; expresses a completely different nature than anything within the physical realm.

We may also note that within each person can be found common inherent social needs, which likewise are pure conscious energies. This ideation has no physical roots, and composes a reality almost in direct opposition to the mind we inherited from our primitive parents. The mindset is described in words as: equality, truth, freedom, peace, love, personal talent and everlasting life. A state of justice is dependent on satisfaction of these personal needs of environmental exchange. There is also the fact that all truths entered our reality from within the personal consciousness of someone. Physical principles are not acquired through the physical senses; are not visible. Human ideals are only applicable to conscious perception; knowledge exists only within consciousness; every perception in the human mind has a REAL source; we perceive not only objects, but a world of thought as well; so as these ideals were not already existent within the human physical realm; indications are a greater consciousness is in our midst; with which we not only can communicate; but most likely is the source of existence for which we search.

The overall scheme of our world is a real-idea interchange. Without an idea, or consciousness the physical world would not be realized, and therefore essentially be non-existent. To realize existence requires consciousness. Without consciousness there is nothing. Having experienced, or realized the elementary mechanics of our physical environment, we know it existed before us. Therefore separate from human consciousness. We also know the physical world is of different substance than human consciousness. Then, it could not be our source. The physical world is governed by steadfast laws, which will operate whether or not an individual is there to perceive it. This would be the case should mankind become extinct. To comply with the overall scheme then suggests for the physical world to exist with or without the presence of human consciousness; a greater consciousness should have been, and still be in existence. You can't have one without another. For there to be an object; there should be a subject. Or maybe we aren't separate at all. Maybe the basic energy from which our world emerged, and our consciousness is somehow an extension of the consciousness of God. The entertainment of any idea of separation could be a primitive remnant.

Within each person is another world. It has no generational beginning or end, but has been an ever present awareness throughout all the eras. A place of equality, peace, truth, freedom, love personal worth and everlasting life; a place of happiness, or justice exists within the heart of humanity. Our history proves our capacity to introduce this pure conscious ideal behavior into our social environment. Unlike the biological theory regarding survival of the most fit, ascent of humanity seems not relative to the most physically powerful, but guidance through these conscious ideals. Once allowance to follow this mind was extended by America, an acceleration of progress ensued like no other period in history. As these are pure conscious ideas, it would seem the identity of the human species exists not in its physical composure, but nature of consciousness. Affinity for, and ascent directed toward satisfaction of those needs could even suggest we are not physical at all; but in fact are conscious beings. The course of humanity suggests we are not only able to copy oppressive actions in the physical world, but also can access an almost entirely different behavioral mentality. The human body can only perceive and copy what already exists, so such a conscious world should be in existence. The problem is it remains buried under a synthetic ego, and reality formed through a physical perspective.

Eyes are machine parts. They do not see. Vision happens within SELF; within personal consciousness. We can only perceive what is; and use that knowledge to create. The problem is there is no longer the perfect human; the body machine has become imperfect. Therefore, perceptions can be distorted, with resultant faulty derivations. Mind is always active, never a void. When we sleep, we dream. The mentality holding ideas as past, present and future; and beginning and ending could be synthetic, merely a human creation. That a person can only perceive what already exists, and that this always happens at a present moment; would suggest the real world is an ever present existence. An almost entirely different mentality should be in existence. And we are part of it, but we continue to be dominated by thought formed by physical appearances. Perpetuate a mental foundation that is wrong through coercive means.

The reason we can't perceive a nothing is that there is only everlasting existence. We only contemplate the idea of coming from nothing because of the erroneous beginning and ending appearance of forms in the physical world, and retention of the primitive mind so formed.

Like the ideals it holds, personal consciousness, or the true SELF defies academic definition. SELF is an entirely different entity from anything physical. No matter what shape the body or physical mind is in, SELF is perfect. Awake or asleep, SELF always receives perceptions, and expects contentment. SELF separated from physical perceptions is simply personal awareness of existence. SELF has no physical properties, but seems a pure unlimited conscious energy. We can't see SELF, can't touch SELF, and can't predict SELF! The knowledge of feelings, abilities and awareness of existence is entirely personal. When you look in the mirror, you see your body. Your SELF, your person, your 'being' is pure consciousness. There is no scientific formula to describe the composition of pure thought, of personal consciousness. It most likely is impossible for the physical body to produce a pure conscious being, or SELF; there must be some other explanation.

Life essentially is a real-idea interchange. The problem is both the body and environment began a descent. Absence of even the tiniest enzyme can alter physical perceptions. Severe isolation compounded the problem. The primitive separation in stations of time, place and person provided only very small pieces of the whole of reality. The human idea, or mind became limited by time-space; and faulty body machine.

There is strong suggestion that humanity holds an inherent need for guidance from a greater 'being'; and everlasting life. Awe and fear are common psychological components radiating from early religious worship. Ancient religions hold a god of variable environmental forces that cause destruction; as the wind, sea, volcano, earth, sun, fire, river, or sometimes a dangerous reptile. The image of a power control system determined by physical power was extended; projected on to an ultimate power. Gods of the ancient world were considered supernatural, but all had human characteristics and physical needs. The primitive vision was limited to immediate physical reflections, and so was the image of their God. That a greater conscious existence would possess such a limited earthy mentality makes no sense. Still, the religious establishment adheres to that image; has never abandoned the concept of anthropomorphism; and anxiously awaits the end of the physical world.

We will never be in our right minds until we learn how to step out of our primitive memories, the basic mental impressions that were made. It is evident this physiologic process of reality formation has been the case in all of mankind; and that the memory retained, continues to dominate social structure. Despite variations in expression, all cultures across the globe are arranged to support physical power. It explains the reason why men, with greater physical strength are favored, and have ruled. Our persistent focus on visible forms, physical power and hierarchy arrangements is the root of unhappiness. This primitive fixation is why truth escapes us. It seems what is real is obscured by this mind of objects, because from infancy our thought is pulled into its basic formation, or foundation.

So, what is real, remains invisible; and without form, even academia discards it. Or else what is real, is transformed, fitted into the reality created by mankind. All seems a masquerade; an illusion.—-' we dress God as a human, sometimes a human religion. A human is a child of this human God; or others see a human as an animal. A person is a physical body; or the more educated opinion, a person is a brain. A corporation is a person. Life is an animated physical form. Heaven is a place where God lives; and we will go to this place when we are dead. The physical ego is the self. Eyesight is our source of vision. Coercion and laws are necessary to control human behavior. The human intellect is the source of good. The objective world is reality. Physical forms are separate existences. The answers are outside; either in the paleontology pit, or outer space. War is the way to freedom and peace'. We really are not thinking clearly!

The primitive ideation most likely is responsible for the manner our democratic format was adopted by other countries, for failure to recognize the true reason for America's rapid ascent. It is also responsible for the delay in realization of the American Dream; and the current subservience to corporate power. There is no concrete explanation to account for the astounding American growth spurt. "We hold these truths to be self-evident, that all men are created equal, that they are endowed by their Creator with certain unalienable Rights—"; independence from an age-old oppressive leadership mentality was the transition. American laws not only gave freedom to the IDEAL mindset within, but are a framework to support its exercise. Ideals as equality, justice, freedom can't be defined; nor can their Creator, or the awesome progress they effected.

American success seems to strongly suggest the mindset of ideals as equality, truth, freedom, peace, love, personal worth, and everlasting life is our true mind. The satisfaction of these needs during environmental exchange is the source of happiness, or justice. This is the mindset that has led America to internal peace and prosperity. The mind was followed initially, and primarily by a people whose conformity was to belief guidance should be received from God through personal prayer. This mindset evoked a sense of responsibility for the welfare of other people. A compatible diversity of talent emerged and proved to be the only really positive energy in an otherwise deteriorating environment. Our direction was away from environmental harm. The most remarkable innovations were in transportation and communication, suggesting compliance with the natural means of growth, which is to share knowledge. This mindset is not the property of any religion or political system, but the intrinsic composure of every human mind. These words are the substance of what has been called our humanity; has proven to be a natural social conscience. The ideation was not acquired from the reality formed by mankind, but in fact conflicts with it; is the reason to introduce justice always requires a fight.

It should be recognized by now that this intrinsic ideation is in fact our RIGHT mind. As the mind was not acquired from mankind, and can't be instructed, or coerced; it seems logical to deduct God is the source of this endowment. These behavioral truths comprise what has been respected as common sense. The idea we are limited is an illusion. We are free conscious agents; restricted not by nature, but by the human establishment. Our way was not guided by the most powerful, but those with personal character strength.

All energy should be directed toward expanding this inner vision through personal meditation. Like all human establishments, academia remains trapped in the age-old mentality. Believes only objects are real, and the mind must be formed. Human intellect is credited for our accomplishments, God is dismissed. Life is an art! Personal consciousness is the innovator, the deliverer of truths. Within each human mind exists an intact perfect self; that all we may need to do is figure out how to nurture and release. We too have an intrinsic knowledge of our environment, but it is a pure conscious possession.

We need to end the masquerade!

The Invisible Person

"WHEREAS ALMIGHTY GOD CREATED THE MIND FREE—"

This beginning of the 1786 Virginia Statute Establishing Religious Freedom was the precursor of American Constitutional liberties.

Physical existence is essentially a REAL-IDEA interchange. A physical mind is a composite of environmental reflections. Of physical sensory perceptions. Because of separate points in time, geographic location and personal anatomic physiology—no two physical minds are identical. But,—that these separate mental states explain a Creator's intent for personal freedom may be entirely wrong! Where there seems no question American success is relevant to allowance for personal freedom; the means may be misconstrued.

Reflection on the human course reveals a somewhat paradoxical circumstance. Allowance for personal freedom did not further separate; but effected a conscious unity. A conformity from which not conventional behavior; but a diversity of talent emerged. Freedom from the restraints of religious oppression seemed to enhance communion of people. The further extension of civil liberties brought people even closer; as evident in the overall American direction toward common welfare. The First Amendment may have opened up a direct personal line to God.

It was the chaos and destructive behavior of separate physical minds that brought social governments into existence. The US Constitution did not free people from government control; but changed the source of authority. Establishment of social governments to control erratic behavior seems the cornerstone of human development. Where increased freedoms could have returned us to a primitive state; instead it brought forth an acceleration of progress like no other period in history. Reason for this occurrence deserves careful consideration. Events suggest what the First Amendment to the US Constitution may have done goes beyond extension of individual physical RIGHTS. This government decision may have indirectly released human potential; because in essence, it was God, who then became a free agent!

A human body through natural mechanics perceives, simulates and perpetuates environmental behavior. The overall environmental view delivered by our physical senses is that of a hierarchy arrangement effected by intermittent deleterious actions. Those that overpower the normal state, and bring things to an end. As in predator-prey behavior;—or physical events as disease, earthquakes or hurricanes.

The physical mind so formed by environmental images has always maintained social dominance. Evident in the overall master-slave human affair; or the manner military or material power determines hierarchy states of social or religious governments. With the simulation even projected to an ultimate ALL POWERFUL God!

Everything in the human mind has a REAL source; is never

blank; always holds perceptions; whether correct or incorrect. The physical principles governing the physical world do not change; existed before we did. Progress is not an ability to do something from nothing; but is utilization of an already existent knowledge; acquired through improved perception. Every human creation uses natural physical principles. Or copies a physical arrangement; as a camera—the eye; computer—the brain and central nervous system; anatomic replacement as a heart valve; or cloning—replication of a physical life form. All inventions use and replicate already existent principles. The formation of social governments; seems a copy of the manner steadfast physical laws regulate environmental conditions.

The idea is projected as though we were nothing, and are evolving into something fantastic. When in fact the scientific knowledge we tediously accumulated always was in existence; as were maybe billions of unused brain cells. Events suggest we may not be going anywhere; but simply awakening to a world, and a human potential that was, is and always will be in existence. History suggests the human problem may be conscious separation from that world. Primitive people were isolated; as were ancient civilizations. Illusory minds diminish; and the REAL world comes into view; as communication improves; allowing us to "come together in thought." Physical principles, or truths arrived from, and are realized within thought. As we assemble these conscious contributions, our reality expands. Where we focus on a theory of physical ascension; there seems more to suggest we are conscious descendents. Almost as though at one time there was but one personal consciousness; or SELF; to perceive a world. Which now exists in conscious pieces. We seem to suffer a perceptual defect directly related to separation from each other. Because—to share thought has been our means of growth. To carefully consider the nature of conscious ascension over the past 200 years may reveal human mental expansion involves far more than adopting the mind of a conqueror!

Where everything in the human mind has a REAL source; freedom is not a component of,—or perception acquired from the physical environment. Unless there were more to human consciousness than a mechanical ability to perceive, and copy the physical world; and more to human reality than the physical world——a concept of freedom should not exist!

This idea of freedom has no physical source, or characteristics. The physical world is one of inter-relationship of matter. Freedom does not fit the overall pattern; and therefore escapes precise or literal academic definition. Freedom is a pure conscious sense! Has relatives as peace, love, equality, truth, personal worth, justice, everlasting life and——God! The mindset could be a vestigial memory. Of a world where power control, or predatory behavior is not known. Where intermittent deleterious motions do not bring things to an end. This negative motion could be the evil that happened. Aesthetics as the feel of a sunrise on the horizon, the light streaking through the trees in the forest, the plants growing in the field—the newborn child could suggest initial body mechanics designed for a world of everlasting beauty. The motions that overpower and bring things to an end could be an environmental change. Conscious incompatibility to these negative changes may explain the existence of psychological defense mechanisms. Unlike the beginning and end range of human mentality acquired from environmental appearance; this mindset of conscious ideals—of conscious needs—has been a permanent fixture in the heart of humanity—throughout all the changing eras. Everything in the human mind has a real source. Characteristics of these words suggest reflection would be from a PURE conscious everlasting world!

THE LONG OVERDUE LETTER

This ideal mindset of which freedom may be the most vital component is an inherent part of conscious anatomy. Seems a natural social conscience, as overall human direction moves towards satisfaction of these needs. Cultivation of these mental roots started long before America. Trace to the most celebrated people in the human course. As Buddha, Mohammed and Christ. The works of all the major religions, and their Golden Rule of behavior; all direct vision away from the physical world to a place deep in personal thought! All surround pure conscious senses. That the body's anatomic arrangement is to deliver perceptions to the invisible person,—or SELF; it would seem natural design is for SELF-CONTROL! Like all the words in this ideal mindset;— the invisible person, or SELF is also a pure conscious sense. Where the science of physics begins to understand the inter-relationship of matter; SELF stands separate. The human element is not found on the periodic table! Not the body; but thought has been the life of our world! There is no scientific formula to describe pure thought. The nature of pure personal consciousness—separate from the perceptions it holds— remains an enigma!

Conscious ideals compose what is aptly called the human "spirit." The energy of our ascent. Surmounting all physical obstacles. Changing social attitudes. Revealing truths. Moving us toward comforts and compatibility. American success is not relative to intellectual prowess or military power; but to the character strength of its founders! The last paragraph of the US Declaration of Independence: "with a firm reliance on the protection of divine Providence, we mutually pledge to each other our Lives, our Fortunes and our sacred Honor."

The American difference is that it separated from the stereotype government style which simulates environmental appearance. Before America, governments were coercive; or formed the minds of the people. In likeness to intermittent environmental motions, these governments become oppressive; rise and fall! As freedom is a pure conscious sense, the only place a person can become free is within thought. And as a person thinks, so moves the body. America was instrumental in that the format suggests it was composed by FREE minds. The frontier our ancestors penetrated exists within thought! The ideation brought forth in The American Declaration of Independence flows from deep within personal character. To further consider the nature of the American government system; along with the progress that followed; could strengthen the concept of creation; and that we received conscious guidance from the Creator!

Physical principles, or environmental truths are not immediate physical sensory perceptions; require personal effort, are only visible within personal thought. Science has now revealed the basic structure of the human body; and planet earth. An arrangement where each cell has a purpose; which it contributes to an organ; which contributes to a system;—one where energy flows from the inside out; and all contribute harmoniously to form the whole. The process of all biological life;—and the ecosystem as well. The government of the United States of America also seems a simulation. Where each person contributes to a community; which contribute to a state; where energy flows from the inside out through a congressional representative; and all contribute harmoniously to form the whole. That we became prolific should not be an enigma. America simulates the intrinsic mechanism of physical life. Though, what seems hidden from view is that it is not the democratic format, which traces to the city states in ancient Greece; but transition was in the generator,—the energy source of this social machine.

Our founders accurately identified oppression, or power control as the source of unhappiness,—of injustice. The US

Constitution is not a steadfast set of rules like those that govern the physical world; but an open door to change and everlasting growth. In essence is a work of art; brings an ideation into our world from another dimension. A common place deep in personal thought! The document is a framework to protect human ideals. A means of SELF-DEFENSE; and opportunity for future SELF-CONTROL! Credence was in an inherent social conscience. In that needs for equality, liberty and happiness were natural endowments from "Nature and Nature's God!"

The laws of personal consciousness differ; in that SELF seems a pure spontaneous creative energy. Evident in that just a rudimentary release of SELF-POTENTIAL soon moved us toward compatibility; and what seemed would be unlimited actualities. Ironically, the physical environmental mind of adaptation is the restraint to SELF-REALIZATION for the person,—and humanity! The physical mind is predatory. Just varies as to degree of harmful effect. This mind is the only deterrent to overall comfort and happiness. Within each person exist inherent needs for equality, freedom, peace, truth, love, expression of personal talent and everlasting life. Satisfaction of these conscious needs of social exchange entirely determines a state of happiness;—or JUSTICE! This ideology could exemplify the WILL of God! The only inhibitory factor to realization of this American Dream may be failure to recognize the nature of our liberty. Further consideration may suggest where our major religions fitted God into the mentality formed by the appearance of the physical world; the American founders seem to have opened the door to the REAL world; a conscious place, separate from the restraints of time and space; to God's world!

Personal conscious attributes can't develop, and needs can't be satisfied in a world where one person has power over another. Each person has identical conscious needs of social exchange;

and basic environmental physical needs. So, it would seem natural for each person to expect another to think and act as he does. All human establishments have primitive mental roots. Based on a hierarchy system, effected by physical power. This is the primary cause of conflict! Because no two physical minds are identical. And there can be no equality, freedom or any conscious or material satisfaction when one overpowers another. A predator-prey system is futile. Victory of the predator is temporary. Eventually every predator falls prey to a greater predator. All leads to an end; to death. That an organism be compatible with its environment is a basic biological principle. Conscious conformity and everlasting life has been the human quest. That this is the case would suggest neither the multiple realities formed by separate points as to time, place and person; or predation was a condition of an original environment.

That America is composed of united states is not unique. There has always been a tendency toward conformity. From primitive tribes to the establishment of a United Nations. Again we have a paradox. While freedom is a need; so must be conformity. Because it has always been the trend; and has decreased internal conflict. Still, conformity to any outside-in mental formation; as in the variable social governing systems; eventually ends. None are able to satisfy the inherent need for justice; which is a personal perception; in itself a frustration; because personal satisfaction already inhibited by the physical elements of time and space; only becomes further intensified by material rules.

What the American government offers is allowance for a transition from physical control, an outside in mental formation; to SELF control, a pure conscious energy flowing from the inside-out. Conformity during the colonial era was to personal character development through prayer. This continued as a primary educational focus throughout most of the 20th Century. In America all religious works were respected, but the Bible was the primary text. As though guided by some invisible beacon, America began an ascent—and soon began to soar! Physical principles, or environmental truths that always existed started to come into view. A personal potential that always existed became activated. Of most significance was the expansion of a capacity, and preference for a behavior contrary to the predator-prey pattern of other animal life. Everything in the human mind has a REAL source. Progress happened because a reality exists beyond the world delivered by our physical senses; which by reaching a greater conscious depth perception, a natural conformity—or cohesion of deepest thought, or SELF—brought into view.

The body automatically delivers environmental perceptions to the invisible person,—or SELF. Christian principles, symbols and art permeated western civilization. The most fundamental event is the unjust condemnation, crucifixion, and return to life of the body of Christ, the son of God. The most basic belief is that the physical world will end; at which point Christ will return; and all believers will be raised from the dead. Christianity like all living things, grew from the inside-out! Christ was a carpenter, from Nazareth; neither circumstance of any social significance. He walked around the countryside talking to people, mostly in parables; and performed miracles. Selected twelve men to whom He gave personal guidance; and were close witnesses to the supernatural circumstances surrounding His teaching and death; which were later recorded in the common script of the era.

This event impacted the course of humanity like no other! The mentality of Christ's era was functioning at little more than the physical sensory level of experience; composed by primarily physical perceptions. Only if the death and return to life of the body of Christ was a REAL occurrence; unless this entirely impossible physical transition really happened; was an actual physical event; a perception delivered by the physical senses; and experienced by multiple people could it have so moved these men to spread the WORD! This event was totally contrary to physical arrangement; and so was the message! The impact was emotional! Penetrated physical minds; reached personal consciousness; evoked character strengths. Instruction was not linear; not a format to follow. All guidance seemed directed at potential to receive guidance from God through personal prayer; to become free from the mind formed by the body and environment; and to love and forgive each other! Again, unless this were an inherent, a natural conscious need and potential; it should not have gained the massive following, and brought forth a behavior contrary to the animal predatory scheme, or released a personal potential to realize and share environmental truths. Where this well may have been the conscious process of our ascent; realization fades. We fail to reach agreement; our vision perhaps dimmed by the glamour of technology; again returns to the material world.

The crucifix once prominent in western homes disappears from view. A symbol that may have reflected more than the worldwide belief throughout all the eras of life after death. From here an ideation radiated that it is wrong to overpower and harm another person; that to come together in thought, through faith in God's guidance all good things are possible; even resurrection of the body. Where the proliferative activity released by the US Constitution may be directly related; it seems to go unrecognized.

Truths are not immediate realizations acquired by the physical senses. A jury deliberates to discern truth in a criminal trial. A student does not immediately comprehend mathematical or physical principles. The establishment has always been resistant to the introduction of truths. Truths begin as a conscious sense; revelation requires conscious effort; are introduced from, and realized within personal thought. Physical senses are mechanical devices that deliver perceptions to the SELF. Much goes unnoticed. The human course shows a deeper penetration of the environment, and SELF is possible. Personal training can improve concentration to more keenly perceive environmental states. The perceptions can be filtered within SELF to ascertain truth. Vision occurs within personal thought! Physical principles, that always existed, came into view; and a human creative potential, that always existed, utilized the knowledge; and directed it toward common welfare. Overall direction was focused on means to protect from environmental discomfort and harm. To heal the sick, and in America—to never wage war except in self-defense; to predict, prevent and warn of impending natural disasters; to understand ecology; and repair our life-support machines. The means, and the greatest area of progress, surrounds improved communication. There was a long held belief that our world was created by a greater consciousness; to Whom through personal prayer it was possible to communicate with; to make needs known. Now should this idea be correct; and it well may be, as prayer was the instrumental exercise of improved personal concentration; these physical principles, and means of direction toward compatibility—would certainly have been known by that Creator!

There is no longer the perfect gas, oak tree or human; so perceptions basically are images taken by; and of a defective physical system. This is not a condition conducive to a progressive conscious evolution. The place truths, or the intrinsic natural arrangement of the physical world arrived from; and are realized is from the intrinsic part of the human mind; from within personal consciousness; and they did not flow down from authoritarian control; but from within the thought of people often low on the social or professional ladder; sometimes from those with only an elementary education. Behavioral truths arrived from, and are also only realized within personal consciousness. All public education and graduation ceremony directed vision to this place deep in thought. Behavioral IDEALS are without physical substance so can't be acquired in the classroom; can't be controlled, formulated or communicated through ordinary means. Compose instead a free and spontaneous common sense, applicable to any circumstance. Personal consciousness is just that; a conscious sense of personal existence; a pure unlimited conscious energy; and deepest thought has proven a natural tendency to penetrate physical appearance and unite; after which the REAL world started to come into view.

That the physical world existed before we did; and that the overall scheme is a REAL-IDEA interchange; suggests an IDEA should have existed before ours. The only place the REAL world can be known is within consciousness. Personal consciousness holds no physical characteristics; has basic emotional needs of a pure conscious nature; to which intermittent physical actions are incompatible. This seems to suggest unlike the body, personal consciousness is not a physical product. That on gaining social freedom, personal consciousness rapidly brought the REAL world into view; and initiated direction toward comfort and compatibility; that character development through prayer was a precedent to this occurrence; would suggest that within each defective body exists an intact perfect self; the cohesion of which could reveal all truths necessary to restore a perfect world.

The freedom extended by the First Amendment prevented government interference with personal religious convictions. Prior to this governments controlled God. Determined God's expectations; enforced them through the Divine Right of Kings. Contrary to the exemplification by Jesus; God was suited in human garments; a ruler to be feared. America began to end this masquerade by moving divine rights to each person. The Bible became the central authority; the conscious navigator. The anti-materialism, anti-establishment, anti-war movements in the sixties seem the epitome of Biblical guidance; and certainly correlate with the teachings of Buddha, and Mohammed; with the common conscious ideals, as freedom, love, equality and peace that have thrived within the heart of humanity throughout all the eras!

To consider the failure of the LOVE and PEACE movements in the sixties, may be a necessary component to future happiness; as these are basic emotional needs, expressions of the heaven we long for! Unlike the biological arrangement where survival of the most fit flows with physical power; in humanity, it flows with conscious character strengths. The mindset of common conscious ideals surmounted all physical obstacles; and determined our course. Survived despite Roman persecution; was preserved for western civilization at the Battle of Tours; became a social allowance after the American Revolutionary War; abolished slavery after the American Civil War; and the FREE world was able to expand after WW II. Direction of humanity was not an evolution of the physical mind; but freedom of personal thought from environmental control. The direction toward realization of social ideals as equality, peace, love, freedom, truth and respect for personal talent advanced; emerged victorious against overwhelming physical opposition. This circumstance would seem to suggest within the heart of humanity exists a supernatural strength; one that can overcome physical power! Or perhaps as everything in the human mind has a REAL source even more; that within our realm exists a consciousness of greater strength, than the evil that has consumed our minds! That personal strength and ingenuity flow from within the SELF; and

SELF is without physical characteristics, and incompatible with power control; and that this direction has essentially brought us from death, to life; SELF could be a product of that greater conscious existence—or God!

The idea that common human conscious ideals exemplify the WILL of God seems further supported by the ineffectiveness of the love movement in the sixties. Progress seems directly related to increased personal freedoms from environmental vision; which formed a natural communion of deeper thought. This common sense released a conscious energy called the human spirit evident in all social confrontations that effected change toward comfort and compatibility. That the effort in the sixties did not follow this pattern of diffusion and success could well be related to an educational transition. Each person arrives on planet earth with a wide-open consciousness. Is given a reality by parents, siblings, peers, educators and environmental experience. By the sixties, identity as a child of a loving God began to fade; education reduced our status to the highest rung of an evolutionary ladder. Our world is one of power transfers. A science vs. religion war started; and power was transferred to academia. Much of the sixties movement toward the world that exists in our hearts may have been dissociated from God. With academia in control, vision moved to the physical world; to the machine. Respect moved from personal talent, and responsibility to God; to intellectual development; and power began to flow with academic credentials. In simulation to the physical machine; a social machine began to activate.

The sixties was a turning point in the human course. The media projected the anti-materialism movement in images of irresponsibility and drug dependence. The cries for love were silenced. As to finalize it; the concept of a God of love was removed from education; from the mainline entertainment and media. Idealists as John, Bobby and Martin were assassinated. And the material world again gained control. The business skyscraper soon replaced the Church steeple as the highest edifice. Our persistent perception that we are not the only life in the universe moved from peaceful angels; to grotesque outer space aliens. We develop the intellectual machine; rather than the PERSON. See a transition in art, architecture, music and morality; with appeal to the intellect, rather than the heart. Confuse physical freedom, with personal freedom. Almost turning our world into a social circus, and releasing predatory behavior. Human ideals are pure conscious attributes. Promotions based on skin color do not constitute equality; because the idea of promotion, in itself projects a natural inequality. Authoritarian guidance is a vital, and respected strength; but for this necessary state to be effective depends on a superiority level of personal talent; which should always be the priority, no matter what skin color, cultural, social economic—no matter what shape the body is in! No human being is "all knowing"; so we need to respect authority; the child is not equal in knowledge to the parent; the parent not to the teacher; not the patient to the physician; a woman is not physically equal to a man. Equality and freedom are not physical attributes; but exist in personal worth!

It may be vital that Americans consider, and reach agreement on the true nature of these ideals on which our Constitution is based; rediscover identity. We should never settle for anything less. Because like America was instrumental in designing a government in likeness to the natural physical structure; so are the founding principles in likeness to a natural intrinsic consciousness of harmonious inter-relationship arranged to provide everlasting existence. So where nations arranged in likeness to physical appearance,—hierarchy systems with status determined by degree of physical power, are temporary,—rise and fall like the world with intermittent predatory motions they copy; the American design, which is in likeness to environmental and conscious truths, determined by "nature and Nature's God" should not fall, because the conscious ideals have been an everlasting part of humanity, and show evidence of being unlimited energies.

We are not equal physically; not intellectually; not in personality;—no two physical minds are the same. The body automatically delivers images, which form a physical mind. Primitive humanity seems to have incorporated these physical images into a social system. Our human master-slave mentality seems in likeness to animal predatory behavior. Were we no more than products of physical evolution; this predatory arrangement should by nature be compatible. That an organism be compatible with its environment is a basic biological principle. In the case of humanity, where the body, or physical mind will automatically follow social behavior to become either an oppressor, or oppressed; we can see that this behavior is incompatible to the welfare of the individual, the society so arranged, the whole of humanity and the environment. That overall direction is to escape from this mentality would suggest the IDEAL mindset, is the inherent, or REAL portion of mental anatomy; especially as this has been the everlasting need, which moves social worlds toward eventual satisfaction, or compatibility; with human predator-prey behavior slowly disintegrating like all myths, as truths are realized.

The issue of science vs. religion; or evolution vs. creationism to me makes absolutely no sense. Simply seems an exemplification of failure to escape the world delivered by eyesight, entirely physical perspective and retention of the primitive power control mentality so formed. It would seem scientific findings in actuality support the existence of a greater consciousness; and coincide with Biblical teachings. Identity of which remains buried in the mental soup of each study. Realization inhibited by the habit of one group seeking power over another! We have an inherent need to unite under one thought; the problem is the physical minds formed by environmental perceptions, which are power control mentalities always remained dominant. Truth, equality, freedom, peace and love only exist within personal consciousness, defy physical definition and instruction. Compose a common sense; an insight. Thought moves the body. Nurture of this deepest thought, these common needs within personal consciousness seems to have happened through prayer. This process was a precursor to American progress, to acquisition of knowledge and resultant innovations.

Scientific focus is on the physical environment. Religious focus is on personal relationship to God. To have a war between these entities seems a logical impossibility. Science accumulates knowledge of the physical body and environment. Religions communicate a personal potential; surround pure conscious entities as equality, truth, love or freedom; ideas without physical characteristics; that are as invisible as their projected source, or God. Our course shows direction toward satisfaction of these common emotional needs; and that realization is related to retreats from the physical world through meditation. This process is of a pure conscious nature; the words hold no academic definition; because they are not of this reality formed by mankind. Physical evolution is an environmental truth! This enlightens as to body, but in no way can dismiss the idea of creation. The scientific method is a means of physical analysis to determine environmental truths. Ours was not a physical, but a conscious growth!

Everything in the physical world is inter-related. An overall scheme where everything comes from something. So, to come from nothing would seem an impossibility. As each person, and humanity entered an already existent world; so do we seem to believe the physical world entered an already existent place. To consider it was separation from physical perceptions, that brought a NEW mind into existence, an ideal mind; which brought a NEW social world into existence; and that it arrived from the 'inside', was based on personal worth, on individual personal reasoning potential; would suggest this concept is incorrect. All progress seems to indicate the physical world did not enter a place; that the source is not 'out there'. Neither did a Creator make things in the manner we get an idea, and bring it into existence. The discoveries in the physics lab rather suggest what we call reality, is in fact an illusion. Some suggest a limitation to energy which curves round on itself, like the global earth. Others feel the physical world is somehow an extension of the consciousness of God. Most likely we can't find solution.

Because the entire perspective of 'begin and end ' is an inaccurate perception. There could never be a nothing, so truth may be we are part of an entirely different reality, an everlasting existence.

Character development through prayer was a precedent to, and accompanied progress. It was after personal consciousness became free from the environmental mind, and allowance to use that mind became a social reality; that the world became a better place. Then, individual talents and our sense of responsibility for the welfare of another person moved us forward at a rapid pace. Our positive direction is relative to conscious,—to attitude changes. Ours was not a physical, but a conscious ascension. The energy flowed from the inside-out,—from a place deep within personal thought. As consciousness changed our world, so could our world itself have come into existence from a greater conscious source.

Religions perpetuate literal interpretations. Scientists search for concrete evidence of our origin. Our failure to reach agreement on the existence and nature of God, or to find physical evidence in the physics lab most likely is because the search is wrong. All seems to indicate the ONE source is of a pure conscious nature, and we are in essence, conscious descendants. The impact of the Bible was on personal character, the message unspoken; realized within. You can't have literal interpretation of entities as love, justice or God, which are indefinable, can't be put in words. Or scientific proof of an idea we have an 'outside' source, if the basic premise is incorrect. Our mentality, and thus reality was formed by superficial environmental reflections. Progress has shown these perceptions so formed were incorrect; and correction came from our ability to penetrate appearance through our deeper ability to reason; that in essence true vision occurs within personal consciousness, or SELF; and that happened when SELF, became FREE, so by nature SELF would seem to be an unlimited entity.

The major divisions of objectivism and subjectivism could be responsible for all 'opposites'. These basic oppositions of thought could explain compatible and incompatible behavior. To consider in depth, we might even get a glimpse of why there is opposition. This too, may only be part of the human predicament, not a true natural state in that it exists only within our world. The existence in which our world entered may not have positive and negative conditions. Objectivism has always been the favored view, and gains in strength with the scientific revelation of environmental truths. Which is understandable, as our course shows 'objects' are the foundation of our mentality, from which we created a social, or common overall reality. Even though personal, religious and secular realities differ, all have a common feature in that they are based on physical objects, and project this mind on to God, as though God were an ultimate human authority; or dismiss God for the same reason, in that a physical God could not be real.

The primitive mind seems to have been formed by the appearance and actions of animated objects. Human behavior seemed little more than a simulation of the appearance of environmental activity. Thought moves the body. It is possible to consider the human master-slave affair, a simulation of the appearance of the animal predator-prey activity, as well as the more physically powerful geological event overpowering the weaker. Ancient reality was dominated by physical thought, or that formed by the body, through the physical senses. Then, at a time when Rome was busy building roads, and means of communication expanded; the formation of thought from a completely subjective source,—or within the 'invisible person',—the SELF; and of a completely subjective nature,—called human ideals was introduced,—we could say by a Jewish revolutionary who claimed to be the Son of God. Within an entirely oppressive reality, a pure subjective IDEATION, that defies definition and means of concrete instruction; IDEAS as equality, truth, freedom, compassion, peace, personal worth,—a different view of justice began to emerge. This completely subjective thought formed a conscious energy called the 'human spirit', brought us to 'life'; and began to revolutionize our world.

We can see when ancient thought was formed almost in complete accordance with 'objectivism', by an object,—the body; and of objects,—the physical environment—there was no social concept of freedom,—and the social hierarchy system was all about power control,—in essence, all were in bondage to a greater physical power. Scientific progress verifies there is no physical freedom, all is inter-related. Survival of a biological form is entirely dependent, on the satisfaction of individual physical environmental needs. Every perception in this human mind formed by objects—the physical body and environment—has a REAL source. To this date, everything we consider REAL is of an objective nature, has form, or physical substance. To consider our course, basic physical structure and human consciousness in its entirety, we can only conclude this concept is incorrect. There must be more to reality than what greets the physical senses,—than the objective world.

There seems to be two basic types of mental formation. The brain will automatically form thought and copy actions in the same manner other organs do their job; as the heart pumps blood, stomach digests or lungs breathe. No personal effort is necessary. This is the mind of physiological adaptation. This mechanical process formed the root of human reality. From here all human establishments grew. The mind seems a simulation of, if we can say the mind that appears to be at work in the physical world. Intermittent external environmental motions overpower the natural state, and cause harm; is oppressive, incites periodic deleterious activity. This mind is selfish, competes for material gain through respect for a hierarchy arrangement, and strives for a superior position on that ladder. Unfortunately like physical forms are temporary, so are these positions and establishments. As the predator-prey system is futile, because each predator will eventually encounter a greater predator, so seems the case with the human oppressor-oppressed arrangement. Coercion is its means of survival and extension. Like the steadfast laws that govern the physical world, it forces conformity to rules and regulations; demands obedience. This established mind resists change, is inhibitory to the introduction of truth. It smothers personal potential; thrives on the other's weakness; on the other being wrong. There are no two physical minds that are identical.

So, they conflict, because each wants to be right. The mind appreciates linear information and direction; routines and structural guidance; and releases habitual and robotic behavior.

This overall interaction does not suggest any separation of mind from body; or subjective thought, from object. This all is connected through a natural physical system, where images, rules, opinions and actions form human thought. A human body seems to be able to function on auto-pilot; can be programmed by the environment, or parental instruction. This 'real-idea' machine is ONE objective entity. The mind, or idea formed by this machine is not subjective. A human physical mind and personality is in essence objective; in that it is formed by physical chemistry, and physical images of objects. The ego is synthetic, an identity given by others; by the social structure. The words and actions it emits can be easily comprehended through the physical senses and human intellectual mechanisms. Nevertheless it still can't be concluded that objectivism is the correct view, because every physical form has a source, and our origin continues to elude us.

Rather than to pursue search for an objective source 'out there', it might be best to consider the manner mankind makes innovations, or creates. Because even though to do so, requires physical elements provided within, or by the 'machine'; and already existent physical principles; still it could direct us to a more logical path. Neither a God with human physical characteristics, whose word is literal, as given in ancient religious works; or a physical world with a limit to energy somewhere out in space, or existing in a nothing, separate from any thing physical, makes any sense. An all intelligent God is not the answer, as to consider God has a brain is ludicrous; as is to consider that a machine can pop out of nowhere, and enter a nothing. Every human invention entered our reality from the same place; from deep in the thought of someone; not from the mind formed by the environment, but from within personal consciousness.

The other human mindset in existence seems almost an opposition to the 'real-idea' mind formed by the 'machine'. This mind, in fact is the 'person'; the receiver of the perceptions formed by the 'real-idea' mechanism. A personal conscious awareness of existence is an EQUAL experience no matter what shape the brain, body or environment is in. Is the TRUE SELF; experiences an emotional state determined by the nature of perceptions received. Personal consciousness is the home where talent resides; from where innovations spring. Physical truths flowed out from, and are realized deep in thought. A need to love, and be loved exists only within personal consciousness. The entire natural intrinsic structure of body and environment seems arranged to support the 'person', or SELF; to provide conscious awareness. The brain delivers perceptions to the 'self', and the primary emotional need is happiness. Vision occurs within personal consciousness. Our history clearly shows 'self' does not like what it sees; and has the ability to escape; to bring a better world into existence.

Personal consciousness is an entirely subjective entity. The energy of our ascent flowed from an entirely subjective generator; from within personal consciousness. We came to life, when energy flowed like in all living things; from the inside-out,—from this inner invisible person. We seem to recognize the visible effect, the tangible objective changes, but not the nature of the source, or the energy. We also fail to identify the merit of these personal efforts; or where they are taking us. Entirely subjective ideas, expressed in words as honor, devotion, love and divine inspiration moved us away from environmental control. Reduced the degree of harm caused by disease and injury; adverse social, geological or meteorological climatic conditions; and oppressive human establishments; most especially governments. In essence what 'made the difference' was a change in social guidance from obedience to human authority; to a God of love through personal prayer. From here a common mindset described in words as equality, truth, freedom, peace, compassion, personal worth and justice became motivators. This mind is not acquired from the physical environment; is an opposition to physical oppressive mentality. This can only be found deep within personal consciousness; and we can't attribute it to cerebral function, because the words can't be defined, or communicated in the usual manner of physical instruction; can't be controlled, or annihilated. These pure subjective thoughts overcame what seemed insurmountable physical obstacles. The mind formed by the body delivers a picture of a physical image of the battlefield, with concrete explanations for cause and victory; but a deeper view suggests otherwise. Our course has been determined by personal character strengths, which are not a part of genetic inheritance, can't be instructed or even comprehended in the usual physical manner; a knowledge we agree exists, but remains enigmatic. The place these pure conscious energies from within are taking us is self-satisfaction.

SELF is the LIFE of our body; and has been the life of our world. Self is entirely subjective, as is personal character; which through an entirely subjective means we sense in another person. Our ascent came from within self, and is directed toward eventual self-satisfaction. The American difference was the release of self-worth through an ideology based on SELF-EVIDENT rights. Not tangible laws, or literal Biblical interpretations; but an entirely subjective Golden Rule guided our ancestors. The frontier they penetrated was not linear; they came together in a common world of justice, which exists only deep within personal thought.

Personal consciousness is not the mind formed by the body;

but the viewer of those perceptions. The source of personal consciousness is not known. A person in actuality seems a pure conscious entity without any physical identity, defies scientific analysis. I feel most likely origin is related to the energy source of all environmental life. To the entirely subjective existence we call God. The underlying factor of progress was social direction of vision away from the objective world, to a place within personal thought. From this source within human consciousness, compatible physical changes began to happen. The positive motion effected by people, who became free from an incorrect physical mind, and oppressive behavior. Only to continue in this direction, to be guided by true consciousness can we find truth, and happiness. All seems dependent on securing FREEDOM from the incorrect mentality formed by the body.

We are at a stage where it should be clear progress was related to personal convictions, and nothing about it was planned, or concrete, but 'just happened'. The similarity in all contributors is personal freedom from physical restraint, or the mind of their era. In essence positivity is when SELF, directs the body. Our history suggests SELF, or personal consciousness to be capable of introducing unlimited actualities; with the only inhibitory factor being physical restraint. There is no reason we can't change our minds. To free self from restraint by the physical mind could lead to an eventuality, where there are no restrictions of time and space. The physical mind with all its ideas of limitations and oppositions may be an illusion; disappear in its entirety. Where it seems now the best we can do is free personal consciousness, allow it to create a compatible physical reality; but eventually pure consciousness may prove to be all there is. Our Alpha and Omega; the place we came from, and to where we return.

Where we gloat because of our intellectual prowess; our mentality may be insignificant to the whole of reality; may not even prove to be real. Every idea in the human mind has a real source, even though the perception may be inaccurate. There has always been an ideation that life forms, other than human exist beyond planet earth. We only change the forms from gods and goddesses, to angels and outer space aliens. From the physical environment came a human body machine; which automatically forms environmental images in a mind; physical forms change, appear to have a beginning and end; thus establishing a human beginning and end mentality range of thought. A totally different reality could be in existence. One that has nothing to do with physical forms; inter-relationship of matter; or beginnings and endings! A conscious awareness may exist far greater than the almost insignificant mind formed by a planet earth machine. To consider humans as mechanical products, certainly makes us artificial. Where there is concrete evidence to explain our physical mind and body, it is not authentic, comes in all sorts of shapes and sizes, and the minds of many historic authorities have faded, unable to endure through the test of time; physical minds seem artificial reproductions of true consciousness. There is nothing to suggest the 'person', the self is not original, is not true consciousness. All contributions to our world from within personal consciousness certainly are original. So, most likely the 'person' is the authentic part of the body machine. An everlasting conscious world may be what is real; and human reality an artificial product manufactured by mankind.

Science holds many contradictions and unanswered questions relevant to human ascension from a single cell in the ocean, to complex biological machines. Should this be the case, why isn't it still happening? Has any one seen any physical body evolve? Any ape-men running around the jungle; any sea creatures transforming to mammals on the beach? Why are lower forms still around? If man were nothing more than a product of earth; why would his psyche differ; why be able to step out of the reality formed by his physical adaptive devices? Why is our basic psychological need for love, and fulfillment of this need not only an individual drive, but that of humanity; a contrast to the overall animal behavioral scheme of predator-prey? Scientific findings show there is no longer the perfect human, gas or oak tree; that energy once used can't be replaced. Does this not suggest the physical world is in a state of descent? Where then does this idea of physiological human ascension come from? Why when there is an intrinsic harmonious homeostatic mechanism of body and environment; is there an outer motion that brings things to an end? Why when the animal world reflects a natural hierarchy arrangement; does human social inequality cause psychological trauma? The science of psychology finds inferiority complexes abnormal, inhibitory to personal ability and happiness. Environmental oppression, from parents, employer, spouse teacher—or loss from natural disaster is the cause of the many psychological disorders. Why would we have a medical profession, care about another's welfare; if we were merely the highest rung of a predator-prey ascension ladder? Why would the majority of illnesses and injury be stress related if oppressive motions were natural? Ecologists find human predatory behavior is destroying the environment necessary for survival. Could not the intrinsic physical homeostatic mechanism; with the intrinsic human conscious desire for everlasting life, suggest "everlasting" was the original state? Why does predatory behavior in humanity threaten extinction; when in other animals, it seems means of survival? The body and environment are presented to children with the ideation they are biological machines. Do not all machines have a creator?

Social inequality is incompatible with basic human nature. Our course shows preference, and capacity for a behavior contrary to other animal life. America is based on belief the mindset of ideals as equality, truth or freedom compose natural social laws, which were decreed by "Nature's God". Awareness and release of this conscious potential was during an era when social focus was on character development through personal prayer. This philosophy initiated a proliferate energy seemingly capable of unlimited actualities. Moved all toward comfort and compatibility. Where oppressive governments before failed; and even afterwards, as the Nazi Regime initiated horrific behavior, and came to an end!

A person is authentic; can't be reproduced. We can't create another Thomas Jefferson, Abraham Lincoln or Martin Luther King; not Ella Fitzgerald or Elvis Presley; not Albert Einstein;—none of our celebrities, no person at all. We can reproduce and train the body; but that may just be smothering the true creative conscious being within. All suggests a world of equality, truth, freedom, peace, compassion, everlasting life—of justice; and talent exists within each person; we just need to figure out how to nurture it; and set it free!

Why Do Bad Things Happen to Good People?

Why do bad things happen to good people? Devastating events bring out this age old question. Then, unanswered it again fades as we resume our daily routine. To consider environmental and behavioral principles in relation to the nature of the human course may provide some ideas worthy of consideration. Common sense deductions can be derived, which may prove the guides toward a long overdue realization of the nature of good and evil; of why devastation exists within the realm of a loving God!

The physical environment holds an appearance of an overall hierarchy system effected by a predator-prey power control arrangement. Tsunamis, earthquakes, floods, forest fires and hurricanes are natural physical events. Humans being a part of nature show similar oppressive actions as kidnapping, murder, terror attacks and wars. Physical disease and death are natural events. The physical world harbors many intermittent motions that overpower the normal state and bring things to an end!

The human body automatically takes an environmental

picture; which seems to form in a physical mind. Thought moves the body. We start as little children to copy environmental actions. This is an automatic process that can continue throughout an individual's existence. It could be construed that our social worlds were so formed. Our reality, or common thought media traces to a primitive mind that was formed and directed by images delivered by the physical senses. The ancient worlds were isolated; the view was limited to local appearance. What an individual would have been seeing at times was a more powerful animal or physical force harm the weaker. To consider the manner a human body machine automatically delivers an environmental image to a person, and the view is copied; combined with inherent desire to live forever, and the automatic survival mechanisms of the body; we can see reason for the 'way we think' and structure of the social establishment. The human course suggests a primitive individual was governed by the body and environment. Despite so-called civilization, the respect for physical power endured. This is especially reflected by events in, and attraction to the Roman arena. A predatory mentality prevailed; with ultimate human-like Gods believed responsible for the natural physical forces capable of destruction. The master-slave human affair; the entire social hierarchy system could have been inspired by environmental reflections.

   Such were the worlds encountered by the most revered celebrities of humanity; of Buddha, Mohammed and Christ. The existence of these people affected our course like no other! The impact was not physical; but emotional! They hold a common accomplishment. Were able to direct vision away from environmental appearance, to a place deep in personal thought! Our strength seems relative not to intellectual, or physical exercise; but to that of meditation. From within personal character, an energy called the "human spirit" emerged, and gained momentum. Described in words as truth, freedom, equality, love, peace, personal worth and everlasting life. These words that defy academic definition surmounted all powerful physical obstacles. Became our navigator; our guides to a conscious place called happiness,—or justice!

A GOLDEN RULE was the educational focus of every major religion. Conformity to this rule did not provoke a robotic conformity, but released a common sense applicable to all personal circumstance. It was not a set of concrete rules to memorize and repeat, but a realization perceived deep in personal thought. From here a human potential and preference to behave in a manner other than predator-prey emerged. The Golden Rule may identify the nature of personal character,—and God! It entirely surrounds behavioral ideals found only within the invisible person, or SELF; and realization is entirely dependent on personal effort. Ideals as equality, truth, freedom, love, justice. personal worth and peace are pure conscious entities. The American founders considered these entities God given RIGHTS! Every thought in the human mind has a REAL source. These ideal behaviors certainly are not copied; are not images acquired from the appearance of the physical world. The Constitution of The United States of America not only opened the door to opportunity for social expression of this ideal mind; but for it to govern.

America was instrumental in designing a social world in likeness to all living things where energy flows from the inside-out! Separate from the world of "mine and yours" exists a "spirit" that is "ours." Through this spirit immigrants from all over the world were able to come together in thought. When conformity was to character development through prayer a natural diversity of talent emerged. Scientific principles, or the REAL world; and true human potential rapidly came into view. Within this knowledge of physical principles, or truths exists the one, and perhaps only human problem. The human body machine adapts to; copies; and chemically perpetuates a behavioral pattern. To consider the historic antipathy between variable cultural groups; or the manner variable local behavioral, or occupational styles perpetuate would suggest in the future, scientists may reveal memories to be part of genetic inheritance as well. What matters is the power control motion that brings things to an end; and the mind so physically formed is incompatible with both the intrinsic nature of man, and his environment.

We find under the appearance of biological life forms, and planet earth exists an arrangement where each cell matters; contributes to a physical part; which contributes to a unit; which contributes to a system; and all contribute harmoniously to the whole; this continuous process is a homeostatic mechanism. In the case of human consciousness, we find under the mind formed by physical appearances exist pure conscious energies called ideals, or the human spirit, from which environmental truths, creativity and compatibility flowed; which also seems to be proving an unlimited and everlasting energy. The government arrangement of The United States of America was transitional in that it does not simulate environmental appearance, but the intrinsic biological and ecological mechanisms instead; and supports not the power control mind formed by environmental appearance, but the inherent mind of ideals. Of interest is this dormant mind once released followed the same basic structure where each person seemed a conscious piece, contributing personal talent and knowledge harmoniously toward welfare of the whole.

It is a biological principle that an organism be compatible with its environment. That this power control motion is incompatible, and contrary to intrinsic arrangement would suggest this negative activity was not an original condition. If there is one thing on which science and religion agree, it is that the physical world is no longer in its original state. There is no longer the perfect oak tree, gas or human; and ecologists have long been sounding an alarm as to diminishing resources. This scientific knowledge available because within this world of physical descent, and where a deleterious motion brings things to an end; we see what appears as a positive motion. It is called human progress; a conscious ascent! It does not make sense an ascent could transpire from defective physical machines, the mind of which is formed by a defective body and environment. Adaptation should be to the environment perceived through physical adaptive devices; to the environment, and by the body in the state they are in. Devastation and harm should be acceptable, or compatible; the natural way! Instead we express antipathy to oppressive actions. The caves are definitely not where we wanted to be! We hold an innate desire for happiness! Satisfaction is dependent on a condition of everlasting well-being and harmony! So it would seem we may be victims of a world gone wrong; but our direction suggests the predicament need not be terminal.

All may depend on whether true human potential will continue to be realized, and remain free. There is a concern. We may have been blinded by the glamour of technology. A roadblock may have been placed in our path. Overlooked seems to be the nature of progress; of the manner environmental truths came into view. Scientific principles are not sensory acquisitions; are not visible to the eye. The place truths are realized, and from where they emerged is deep in personal thought. Words as compassion, divine inspiration, honor and devotion surrounded the search for and the utilization of truths. These conscious energies also escape the physical senses. We may not be physical ascendants; but conscious descendents instead. Within the human brain exist what may be deactivated cells once capable of transmitting a world beyond even our present ability to imagine. The primary avenue on which we embarked continuously moves us toward improved communication. "To share thought" has been our means of growth! The culprit interfering with the realization of truth is the limited mind formed by separate points in time, geographic location and personal physiology.

The reason for progressive social changes is that a knowledge exists beyond the immediate view delivered by our physical senses; which we have the conscious capacity to perceive; share; utilize to create; and direct toward common welfare! Where we have become awed by what we consider intellectual prowess; our direction seems only an effect of American opportunity to follow our common conscious sense. This seems to be providing a slow escape from conformity to the erroneous mind history shows was formed and enforced by human establishments. Contributors of physical truths encountered ridicule and resistance; for some there was severe punishment as especially evident in the behavioral truths released by the original followers of Christ. Truth always survives; is everlasting; can't be annihilated; and seems to have its own way of being known. Our ascent was not effected by the mind formed through natural physical adaptation. Truths escape physical sensory detection. Truths are not automatic perceptions. Require time and effort to realize deep in thought. Truths arrive from, and are realized deep within personal consciousness. Environmental truths and innovations came from people often low on the social and professional hierarchy ladder. With some of the greatest contributions emerging from the thought of those with only a grade school education,—without any academic credentials! Our ancestors were artists; had no blueprint to follow. Once a truth is realized, or agreement is reached; the establishment incorporates it into the ancient power control system. Thus maintaining the illusion 'all comes down from above'. Having not escaped from this illusion is why the thought persists that a God "above all" causes, or allows devastating events to happen.

The current consensus that religious teaching is not a secular need deserves careful consideration. The physical body is a biological machine. Holding a primary purpose. To deliver perceptions to the invisible person,—or SELF. Eyes are machine parts; eyes do not see. Vision occurs within the SELF. This basic fact suggests natural arrangement is for SELF-CONTROL! Separated from physical perceptions, SELF is pure consciousness. There is no scientific formula to describe the substance of pure personal thought! Scientists have not yet uncovered the nature of this mystical entity known as a PERSON. The brain, physical mind and body chemistry can be analyzed. The data used to improve physical function. Chemical changes can alter physical behavior; as can social rules. This improves a person's body, and allows conformity to a social environment; but despite benefit, in no way involves any alteration of the receiver, or person.

Reflections on the human course suggest personal consciousness was touched, or activated through prayer and meditation. This was a precedent to realization of our current level of scientific knowledge, the principles of which in actuality always existed, or were available. To which we were blind, did not see. We were guided to awareness of human anatomical and physiological principles by the conscious energy of compassion. The physical truths were needed to ease suffering. This was the purpose of pursuit, and end to which the knowledge was directed. That scientific breakthroughs happened during eras where focus was on personal character development through prayer: makes it very possible the guidance came from the Creator of this knowledge; that this Creator exists; and to whom through deepest thought we can communicate. God was the common denominator of social life. God could well be the entity from where the common sense that directed personal actions emerged. Through Holy Communion, Christians came together in deepest thought. All religions have communal prayer; and encourage personal meditation. Prayer is related to the improved personal perceptive ability of humanity. Physical principles came into view during eras where the Church was the highest community edifice; and prayers reached a place deep in our heart. Ideals guided our intelligence, and the knowledge was utilized to protect us from physical harm. Separation from truth is the human obstacle to harmony and well being. Our course seems little more than a tedious realization of the REAL world, and REAL human potential.

The spread of a common ability to perceive a JUST God was the forerunner of the physical truths that flooded our world, and enhanced our reality over the past two centuries. This could suggest the most fundamental natural principle, or TRUTH is not of a physical; but of a conscious nature; a SELF-potential to access knowledge in a manner other than that derived by physical senses or earthly intellectual mechanisms; that the knowledge so derived is composed of physical and behavioral truths; the utilization of which dramatically improved our state of well-being; would support the concept that the communion of our innovative predecessors was indeed with a very real conscious existence; with God—our Creator! The nature of the realizations could further suggest this consciousness, or God has NO physical characteristics; that the knowledge in fact is a direct contrast to the physical mind of our primitive ancestors, and the appearance of earthly forms and actions; and recognize our conscious simulation; which has been expressed through the behavioral ideals; ability to perceive a knowledge beyond that delivered by automatic body mechanics; and to use this knowledge to CREATE! Truth is not a physical; but is a conscious entity! Truths are realized deep in thought! Our separation from truth exists within personal consciousness. Consciousness is the living growing thing! Successive generations inherit not a better physical world; but a closer proximity to truth. As though within each defective physical mind, exists an intact perfect SELF, or personal consciousness; that where our physical separation causes knowledge deficits, which lead to conflict; this deepest thought expresses an affinity, or by nature moves toward cohesion; effecting academic agreements, or TRUTHS, which lead to harmony.

Especially exemplified by the difference in conformity to social rules, including those of the religious establishment; compared to social conformity to the belief personal guidance could be received from God through prayer. Where theoretic education, and rules of human authority lead to a robotic conformity; which cause variable groups to conflict, as especially evident in political parties; social conformity to encourage and allow proximity to God through personal prayer released a DIVERSITY of talent, and an energy seemingly capable of unlimited potentiality; which blended harmoniously, as in the American "melting pot." Evident in the difference in political guidance then; and now. When God was dominant, differences melted toward common welfare; where now after a primary educational transfer of respect to the human intellectual machine; one political opinion seeks instead to overpower the other; engulfing minds in the same manner as Nazism, communism, fascism—or any other outside-in government design. When we arrive on planet earth, we enter not only a physical world; but a world of thought as well. Are taught basics as this is a tree, house, parent and so forth; a language and cultural behavior; are disciplined to conform to social expectations; are exposed to prejudices; acquire a political party preference; a national heritage of government philosophy; a theoretic education; and obedience to the rules of a particular religious establishment. An individual mind forms accordingly; and these minds conflict. Because each person, or human establishment wants their view to be held by everyone; to be TRUTH! We can deduct from this natural inclination, that it would not be the case, unless indeed ONE TRUE reality does exist; that we are common inhabitants of a REAL world not yet perceived. Each person with a normal physiology through natural adaptation to environmental conditions acquires a physical mind. The combined thought called reality. However, these worlds so formed could not be reality, because truth is steadfast; and these worlds differ, and change throughout generational eras. We no longer exist in the world of our primitive ancestors. Neither the physical world, or social world is the same. From the American experience we may be able to see these changes are not brought forth because we are physiological ascendants with superior intellectual capacity; but because we are more than biological machines!

The Constitution of The United States of America in essence is a work of art! Our ancestors did not have a blueprint to follow; but were artists! The recent linear focus incapacitates its potential. As religious works guide the reader to SELF realization, potential and satisfaction; so does our constitution open the social door to expression of the inherent ideals so acquired, or developed through SELF introspection and analysis. The entire process seems to explain the nature of personal, and social maturation. No government constitution, or religious doctrine can give concrete direction, or rules to guarantee justice, or happiness. The invisible person, or SELF seems a pure conscious energy. While we focus on the physical environment and body; we tend to overlook the fact that although the physical world is a vital life-support machine; SELF is the LIFE of our body,—of our world! A REALITY is SELF created! People have common physical and social needs. The inhibitory factor to common satisfaction of these needs, or happiness is a physical world harboring intermittent deleterious actions; and a social simulation of this oppressive activity. As an organism must be compatible with its environment; and this activity is incompatible; that our ascent has been through pure conscious energies called IDEALS, not acquired from physical images, but from meditation; from deepest personal thought; which has revealed physical principles necessary to predict, and prevent catastrophe; that the most primary, and foremost element of progress exists in improved communication; suggests we are not primarily physical machines; but are conscious beings; that this motion that brings things to an end is not part of our natural heritage; that separate from this negativity earth supplies the physical and aesthetic needs; and displays an intrinsic homeostatic mechanism; suggests it is the natural physical oppressive activity which is not part of our original environment; that to comply with an overall natural pattern; for these needs to exist, so must means to satisfy them; and our history seems to reveal that the means exist within each personal consciousness,—or SELF! That the nature of personal consciousness is not of the same substance as physical forms would suggest there is still a part of mental anatomy to be identified. Where the physical mind acquired from our predecessors remains dominant; it should be noted that social and academic changes toward truth and compatibility emerge not from this acquired mind, but from deep in personal thought. Would suggest SELF, or personal consciousness which is not understood by current human academic authority should be considered our most prized social possession; and that it well may be a necessity to return to prayer for continued personal maturation to comply with the natural arrangement for personal character maturation, or SELF control. Where SELF is by nature a free agent with unlimited energy, and the home of a natural social conscience; like the physical world is controlled by natural laws; so is the physical mind limited to intellectual program; as these are variable, freedom separate from true self-control through prayer could lead to ultimate chaos!

Personal character development through prayer was the focus of all religious works and instruction. To which there was secular respect and compliance. Until the sixties, encouragement of personal prayer was a primary secular focus. A sense of personal honor, and the value of personal talent accompanied theoretic education. Secular entertainment and news media included God in their presentations. There was not only respect for natural laws of personal consciousness, but adherence to this "common sense" a social demand. No two people share physical equality. Each person does have equal access to God. Has equal potential for personal maturation through prayer. Church and God are not analogous. Churches, although each based on a Common Divine Root, are human establishments holding conflicting academic opinions. The unspoken message of all major religions, the substance of SELF and God may well be one natural entity. To end encouragement of personal proximity to God could well prove an interference with natural law. An action which always produces undesirable effects.

Our humanity is not evident in intellectual prowess; but in common personal character traits. The propensity to establish a state of justice surrounds ideas as equality, truth, freedom, peace, love, personal worth and everlasting life. Not an academic ideology; but this common personal mind-set—entirely atypical of animal predator-prey behavior—moved us toward unity! We focus on our physique and its similarity to apes; where it is not our body, or the mind of physical images formed by the body; but the receiver of those perceptions; the person, the SELF that is the LIFE of the body; and from where flowed the energy of our ascent. The frontier penetrated by our ancestors was not linear; but exists deep in thought! We now are building an intellectual, and vast social machine. With feet planted firmly on the ground, further ascent is improbable.

The Bible was the navigator of western civilization. The impact was emotional. An unspoken message was transmitted that provoked a change in attitude; enabled greater conscious depth perception. Ours was not a physical, but a conscious ascent. Personal maturation and character strengths emerged. The overall scheme of human existence is that of a REAL-IDEA interchange. A REAL, or objective environment; appears in the IDEA, or consciousness. Human reality is clearly a world where what is considered REAL started with the appearance of physical forms, and despite the fact this appearance was an illusion, and that all truths and innovations emerged from an idea that established authority believed to be ludicrous, has only progressed to the point where: there must be physical evidence to support whether an idea is REAL. The physical environment and human body is ONE mechanism, of which the human mind is a product. This seems to infer the mind so-formed is not REAL, but synthetic,—manufactured by the body and environmental machine.

This synthetic human mind is not the IDEA,—not human consciousness. The 'person',—the SELF,—the receiver of perceptions,—the holder of a physical mind—is consciousness. We have made great strides in revealing truths relative to the human body and physical environment,—the REAL; we also gain access to knowledge of the source of the human body and its intrinsic mechanisms; but the source of the whole physical mechanism remains an enigma; the IDEA,—personal consciousness,—the true SELF,—the 'person'—escapes recognition,—continues as a complete enigma. This is because our perspective,—is determined—by elements and mechanics— all within the ONE real-idea mechanism,—by the physical mind and environment—which is what we believe to be real,—so all thoughts flow through this picture;—a mental image of a global earth, which some theories even suggest the energy of which may extend into the universe and curve round on itself, hence making the picture of a global physical universe;—existing in a NOTHING,—in essence an appearance of isolation is the effect;—as we know there must be more, because everything comes from something, we deduct separation;—the same with the human mind, as each individual physiology differs,—each mind differs giving the 'person' within an image of separation,— which becomes further encapsulated within this physical mental barrier.

The last century clearly demonstrates our innate intelligence. Why then is there no scientific explanation for the origin of the physical world? Why is there no theological or philosophical deduction that is accurate? There seems only one answer that would explain why we can fly to the moon,—but not find solution to the enigma of life. It could only be that although intrinsic knowledge of the physical world is truth,—the overview,—the picture of the box,—the mental foundation,— the physical perspective limits our thought,—and our reality. Simply put,—what we believe to be REAL,—other than intrinsic truths,—is NOT. Natural arrangement is for the body to deliver perceptions to the 'person',—true self,—or consciousness; suggesting original function was self-control; instead thoughts and action are determined by the physical mind,—which in essence means we are under environmental control. Mankind is not in its right mind! This, and only this may be what separates us from reality!

The environment existed before we did; then to comply with the real-idea arrangement; so should have consciousness existed before us. Reflections on the human course suggest bad things are not caused by God; but by separation from God. Prayer to a God of LOVE was a precedent to progress. We came together in deepest thought, and unknowingly seem to have embarked on a common purpose. To escape from the deleterious actions of the physical environment, and the oppressive human establishments formed in its image.

The human predicament seems to exist in our natural mental formation. Our separation from God has nothing to do with time or space; but everything to do with personal thought. The basic emotional needs we call ideals may be vestigial memories from an original compatible environment. We enter not only an already existent physical world; but an already existent world of thought. Human communication involves more than words and actions. A sense of justice accommodates daily experiences. This is what matters! Our happiness at the end of the day is entirely dependent on just behavior. There are no concrete rules to follow. Life is an art! Like physical principles existed right in our midst without our awareness; so may God.

Our ancient ancestors existed in a world that was flat! Because they relied on a mind mechanically formed by physical senses. We reached a greater conscious depth perception, and now vision—or live on a global earth. Still we may be far from truth;—from home! We continue to view ourselves as physical bodies; and the power control environmental appearance as though this was made, or intended by God. Religions have primitive roots; thus brought God into the mental world made by man,—or human body mechanics. Dressed God in human clothes. Gave God a physical location. A distant home somewhere within the world of time and space. We view God as a physical man, and His Creation as something brought forth in the same manner as human inventions, and like it is some sort of selfish possession. Scientists have pretty well erased this human-like picture of God. We are so focused on the mental world made by man, and his environment; that God remains invisible. We are more than humans. We are human "BEINGS!" There is no scientific understanding of personal consciousness; or the sense of justice that flows through people. This is the God that has endured throughout the ages, and can't be disproved. It is possible that in similarity to the manner science students envision invisible physical principles; uncounted millions envision God through prayer! All we may need to do to enter the TRUE world,—God's world,—is end the masquerade!

To establish a state of justice is not a propensity of the mind acquired from the reality man has created through physical adaptation to a predatory environment. The world of equality, truth, freedom, love, creative ability, peace—of everlasting life—exists within our personal thought. Adaptation to social standards is not entirely natural; but coercive. Should we no longer be taught that we are white, red, yellow or black; rich or poor; worthy or unworthy; German or Chinese; Christian or Mohammedan;—are something separate from all else; most especially that we are right, they are wrong; that one idea is good, the other bad; we just might be able to find truth; and discover there is only good. We force obedience either to a God with a physical finite mind,—or to scientific theory; look 'out there' for a ONE source of human existence. Our course shows the effect of the Bible was on personal consciousness, had an emotional impact, which released character strengths, and a deeper conscious awareness. Quantum theories of inter-relationship suggest our reality founded on the appearance of separate objects is an illusion. All seems to suggest the ONE source is within, and not a physical object, but a conscious awareness, buried under a mentality that is incorrect.

When in America children became free from control by religious authority, but coercion toward personal prayer, and religious works continued, a universal spirit began to direct social affairs. The American Constitution allows change, is subject to the WILL of the PEOPLE. The dawning of America and following Constitutional Amendments coincide with personal recognition of inherent social rights. Personal character strengths were the human elements guiding our way. A sense of responsibility for the welfare of another person was a primary motivator. This energy from within, or insight moved us from environmental harm, or 'evil'; toward truth and compatibility, or 'good'. So, it would seem 'bad' only existed because there was an absence of 'good'. Then to nurture and release our 'humanity', or this inner vision where 'goodness' exists would seem the direction to assume. To adhere to this inherent social conscience is an equal potential. For each person to contribute their talent to the whole, is the natural means to escape from environmental harm. Social guidance toward personal recognition and obedience to these inherent conscious principles will bring forth a prevalence of good. Until then, 'bad' things will continue to happen to 'good' people. We are all in this together!

The Real World

Each infant arrives on planet earth with what appears to be a wide-open consciousness. This may not be true in its entirety. Scientists are making progress, but understanding of the human mind is still rudimentary. Anatomic exploration of the brain and very complex physiology and chemistry of the central nervous system is all relative to physical function. There is no explanation for personal consciousness, or the common need for happiness in a world where all will suffer to some degree. It is also curious that personal emotional and physical trauma is caused not only by physical environmental changes, as disease or climatic events; but by other people. This would make sense if the human mind was only an evolutionary physical product; but the deepest need is to love, and be loved. Satisfaction of this need is the primary component necessary for happiness. Compassion for others is not only a respected individual trait; but has guided the human course. Human conscious evolution is toward satisfaction of what seems a deep need to 'help each other'. To do so has proven to be in the interest of the whole of humanity, as from deep within personal consciousness came the ideas that have moved us toward comfort. Transformation of a progressive idea into a real entity required support, and help from others. In essence, our progress was brought forth by increasing circumstances of personal separation from an oppressive mentality. Common sense would lead us to derive then; that the mind acquired by the body is not compatible with personal character; and that within each person is the ability to correct this human circumstance. It is also evident that a 'person' is neither an acquired physical mind, nor social label, not even a specific gender. Indications are a 'person' is a pure conscious entity, and is wide-open; but from birth already holds hereditary mental traits.

A mind is acquired through interaction of our body and environment. The body and mind are not separate, but one physical entity. A brain forms thought in the same manner any organ does its job. Lungs breathe, a heart pumps blood and a stomach digests separate from any personal involvement. Physical existence is primarily a real-idea interchange. A physical world is transformed into thought by the brain and sensory devices. An infant enters a world where molecular structure is arranged to appear as forms, which become detectable to the physical senses. A human body is one of these forms. As thought is a product of the body, then each infant enters not only an already existent world of physical forms, but of thought as well. To adapt to, or acquire this already existent thought is a paramount discipline in child education. It is also evident that not only does the body provide an individual with environmental movies through the sensory mechanisms, but it copies the view. This is especially evident in little children imitating others in their environment. Normal mental acquisition then places each individual in a common place. A child acquires a mind in likeness to the common thought projected by an immediate environment. To reflect on our course though shows these mental places brought into existence by the body have not been compatible with inherent personal needs for entities as compassion, truth and justice.

Our progress is evidence there is more to existence than is detectable to the physical senses. And there is more to human consciousness than the ability to perceive the appearance of a physical world. When an individual body machine malfunctions, physical perceptions will be distorted. The person may hallucinate, see things others do not. In likeness to individual experience while asleep, some individuals have the dream while awake. We say this person so affected, has lost contact with reality. This consideration may deserve careful analysis. The key to enlightenment could exist within this concept. Humanity may be in a similar circumstance. The human predicament where life remains an enigma suggests indeed an overall loss of contact with reality!

There are several things to consider when we say the person has lost contact with reality. To begin, it tends to imply individual existence is something in addition to physical mind and body. It is the 'person', who is affected by this body malfunction. The natural arrangement is for the body to deliver perceptions to and from the 'person'. There is no scientific formula, or explanation to describe this pure conscious entity, we call a 'person'. Therefore, we can't be certain of the precise manner this 'person' is attached to the body, and physical environment. All indications are that a person is the holder of physical perceptions, because even though the perceptions are inaccurate, a relative response to the distorted message will occur. I once observed a man standing in a noisy large room filled with other people, who believed he was fishing. The fisherman's actions were so precise; it was difficult to imagine the rod and reel were not in his hands. Distorted perceptions become very real to an individual. To convince these people the delusions are not real is next to impossible. Psychiatric disorders seem to clearly demonstrate the mind is formed by the body, and response will vary according to the nature of the perceptions. Complexity enters in that responses are also relative to individual 'personality'. The images held by this mind are not only of the environment, but of a 'self', or a 'person'. This 'self', called 'ego'; is also formed by the body and environment. No two people have the exact same physiology, or environmental experiences. Therefore each individual has a unique personality, which becomes expressed in diverse and unpredictable ways.

Every thought in the physical mind is relative to the reality created by mankind. Hallucinations describe things within our reality. Even if the individual is seeing pink elephants; the color pink and elephants are both part of our reality; they just don't happen to go together. I think it is even fair to consider in the cases where the individual hears or sees God, to be within our reality; because God has always been described as a man you can talk to. Even though this is part of human reality, there is no evidence to support its validity, so these cases are often significant signs of pathology. Insanity is a state when a 'person' is not receiving accurate perceptions because of physical failure. When the body machine is not working, the 'person' becomes severed from the common place normal body mechanics take us. We call this common place where thoughts relative to a physical environment are formed by a normal body machine,—'reality'. This seems correct, as the real-idea interchange is in actuality one mechanism that forms a view, a mind for mankind.

However despite physical malfunction, these people never become separated from the common 'personal' place we live. Each still holds the expectation of experiencing 'fairness' during daily encounters. Satisfaction is dependent on personal perception, or sense of entities as equality, peace, compassion and honesty, or truth. Therefore, it would seem in essence each individual has two basic mindsets. A human being exists in a 'visible reality' formed by body and environment, composed of physical objects; and also a common 'invisible reality' existing deep within personal thought, where a sense of justice determines contentment. The world in our hearts never changes. Exists in the infant and the aged; the developmentally disabled and the insane; in every race and culture; and has not only thrived throughout all the ages, but moves the social world toward its satisfaction.

This basic component of conscious anatomy, which in actuality should be considered our most prized possession exists almost without recognition. The words bellowed throughout all progressive social revolutions; but comprehension remains clouded. The entities appear in an abstract form, seem of an entirely conscious nature and escape academic definition. With reason most likely being, intellectual understanding, including vocabulary is relative to, and traces to a human reality based on objective environmental appearance. Unlike the content in our physical mind, ideas as equality, truth, love or freedom have no organic roots, are not visible in the environment. Likewise personal consciousness has no physical composition, so is almost ignored. The focus of study is on the brain and physical mind; on what is visible, or objective, and within the tangible reality created by mankind. We remain in a state where personal consciousness can be noticed only as intermittent abstract awareness of personal existence; and our most fundamental emotional need for justice as an abstract social sense. The mind acquired from the environment is of an oppressive nature; and so it seems also to behave in an individual; overshadowing the true self,—the 'person'. What deserves consideration is that where the physical mind is imperfect, often composed of inaccurate perceptions, and can become severely inflicted by faulty body mechanics;

personal consciousness escapes this distortion. Personal consciousness is simply an awareness of existence. This awareness exists in a dream, in the insane and disabled. Interpretations of pain or pleasure are variable, and therefore most likely occur in the physical mind. True consciousness, or the 'invisible person' is not altered by physical changes, and therefore the possibility exists it may not even be altered by physical death. Neither is the 'personal need' for justice altered by faulty body mechanics. This too is a steadfast conscious law, always present, no matter what shape the body is in. Buried under a synthetic reality seems to exist an intact perfect person and reality. Our conscious connection exists deep within personal thought. All that may be needed is to release each 'person' from an oppressive physical mental restraint! To recognize the reality formed by the primitive body machine, and perpetuated by the human establishment is the inhibitor; the divisive factor.

We can see that on an individual basis, the natural condition is one of variable physical circumstance, and personality. Therefore even though the mind is formed in the same manner and from the environment, no two human minds will be identical; and neither will be the mind of two nations. Throughout history and in personal experience, it becomes evident this circumstance of nature is incompatible to what appears to be an inherent need for each person to hold the same view, or the same mind. A human mind is formed by the body and is relative to the environment, or things that are 'out there'. A natural sequence of human mental formation could have started with isolated primitive individuals 'copying' the environmental images delivered by the body. Individual variation would result in chaotic behavior; which again we can see, was not acceptable to the whole. Social groups introduced rules in attempt to establish conformity toward compatible behavior. Then an individual mind became formed not only by a physical reality, but a social reality as well. In the same manner individual minds conflicted; groups of similar mentality also conflicted with others. This conflict led to wars, and afterwards minds blended; knowledge was shared. The conqueror most always forced its social reality on to the defeated. An overview of this repetitive circumstance seems to hold an implication of eventual intent for one mentality to rule mankind. Despite individual variation, this was the method of all religious and secular groups. The government of The United States of America interrupted that pattern. This system allowed conformity through the 'natural' inner 'personal' connection; which released a constructive and compatible diversity.

Historians tend to direct our focus on details of style in variable groups of people that have formed across the globe throughout the course of civilization. To instead consider the overall style will reveal but two distinct mindsets, which are in fact in opposition to each other. Natural arrangement is for the body to form a mind through the physical senses. These sensory devices provide a superficial view; or are only reflections from objects. This mind provided by body mechanics seems to make existence comparable to a movie in which the individual is a participant. The view to a primitive human would have been proximal, or relative to sensory information from activity in a particular setting. No matter what geographic setting, normal physiology would make the individual a participant in a movie where physical power determines survival. We see this natural adaptive physiological mindset prevails throughout ancient civilization. All social structure seems a simulation of environmental hierarchy arrangement based on degree of physical power. The concept of God seems an extension of the view where all physical objects come from something; from some prior existence. In some cultures the most powerful environmental forces became gods; as a volcano, sun, wind or river. Others projected the ultimate power, or ruler on to an invisible entity. All possessed human physical traits and needs. Some of these gods could become visible; even talk to people. These gods held an oppressive nature; with supernatural powers that could cause devastation; could bring things to an end. Humans rightly feared these rulers. The power of raging waters, winds, fires; of volcanic eruptions or earthquakes; all disturbances in the normal environmental setting surpassed human understanding. It is possible to understand why primitive humanity would consider the existence of a supernatural being; and to view this being as a greater predator.

Intermittent destructive natural events appeared to be insurmountable obstacles to our primitive ancestors. The physical mind, body and environment are parts of one mechanism, so to gain physical knowledge seems a natural course. As increased 'scientific' revelations pour in, we transfer allegiance from a supernatural being, to human intelligence. Physical principles are facts; are truths. Human intelligence is a physiological mechanism, an adaptive device. Natural arrangement of body automation is to acquire information from the 'outside' environment. Explaining why coercion has been a successful method of human leadership. A human infant is entirely dependent. Its nourishment and guidance arrives from the 'outside' world. This is true not only for an individual, but also for humanity. Our primitive ancestors formed a reality from the 'outside' environment; the foundation of which continues to encapsulate our thought to this day. The manner in which an occupation, profession, community, nation; or humanity itself thrives; is relative to the nature of the elementary guidance given by generational parents. To be dependent on an 'outside' authority is a normal and necessary human physical state.

Coercive laws in all cultures included what were believed to be behavioral demands of a supernatural being. Overall conformity was toward the encouragement of an individual to receive guidance through meditation. This supernatural being was pretty much owned by a local religion; masqueraded in variable costumes designed by religious hierarchy; as were particular ceremonial practices. The only supernatural quality of a deity seemed to exist in its invisible nature; and ability to change physical conditions beyond that of mankind; as beginning with of course, the ability to 'create' a physical world. Our transition from 'belief' in a supernatural entity, to human ingenuity, as concrete evidence of physical structure became realized; most definitely seems a normal process of physiological adaptation and maturation. However to dismiss the concept of God in its entirety from public education and media may have been incorrect. To only consider the physical facts seems an oversight. The affinity for, and conscious connection to this God of love, which guided western civilization toward success is also factual knowledge; just not visible, has no physical substance; evidence should be considered apparent in the nature of progress. If truth is to be ascertained, we can't bury a fact; especially a pure conscious fact, when the issue is the invisible enigmatic 'personal consciousness and God' affair.

The deduction human intelligence moved us forward is factual, and relatively easy to comprehend because it is relative to what is visible. Every human innovation seems a copy of some natural principle already in existence. Telecommunication resembles the process a human brain transmits messages. These messages have steadily become more linear over the past forty years. A human brain and complex nervous system compose a physiological transmitter. To communicate messages from the proximal area of an individual; from the physiological body and environment is an automatic function. The natural physiological arrangement is for the environment to provide a reality, and satisfy individual needs. Correlation in the case of an individual human is provided by the body; is the brain's job. Provided physiology is normal, accurate transmission should provide a satisfactory inter-relationship. That this is not the case seems indisputable. Many so-called realities have come and gone. These realities, in likeness to the images of biological forms they simulate, have been temporary existences. Reliance on, and primary focus on development of the intellectual machine may prove inadequate. The precedent to progress was an education surrounding personal character. Conformity was toward expression of behavioral traits not acquired from environment, but within the person; as fairness. The physical appearance of our ascent may again delude us from truth, in the same manner an erroneous mentality was formed in early humanity.

The brain specializes in transmission of physical perceptions. Physical responses are relative to normalcy of selective areas delegated by nature for a specific function. Pathology in a specific area will disrupt function, as a stroke may impair the area for speech, co-ordination or even personality. We don't need to delve into neurological anatomy to recognize that brain fibers are selective tissue that responds according to information received. What we tend to overlook is that information is not only transmitted by the physical senses, but a conscious sense of entities that are abstract, or invisible as well. In fact, all transmissions are delivered to and from an entirely abstract entity called a 'person', which is pure consciousness. The primary function of the entire physical mechanism surrounds conscious appreciation. The real obstacle our ancestors faced was not the deleterious natural events, but the psychological effect. Even though a predator-prey motion appeared to be the 'way of the physical world', and humans have a natural attachment to the environment through mind and body; to see things overpowered, to come to an end is incompatible to the receiver of these perceptions; to the 'invisible person' within.

Each person has an intrinsic almost undetectable sense he/she is perfect. The reason this perfect person is buried so deeply could be because that is exactly where the social system forces it to stay. The best indication of this perhaps vestigial conscious awareness most likely is the statement "I can't believe I did that." This suggests it is impossible I could have done such a stupid thing; I'm perfect! There is no perfect human body; no perfect physical entity. Everything has deviated from original perfection. Things are not in their original state. The primitive human mind was formed by an imperfect physical mechanism. The social mindset formed by primitive humanity is a simulation of the appearance of environmental actions. It is a hierarchy arrangement where status is determined by individual degree of physical power. To rise on this ladder is dependent on obedience to rules sent down from above, and ability to enforce these rules. People go along with it, seemingly trapped in the illusion 'all comes down from above'. Deep down inside they know there is a better way. Together they discuss matters. Injustice reaches a common sense. They detest oppression. Revolution by revolution; innovation by innovation; tediously the world becomes a better place. The journey was not planned, holds no exact explanation, travelers well may have been guided by an intact perfect 'SELF'.

The natural physiological mechanism is for the body to deliver messages to and from the 'person'. This implies natural arrangement is for the 'person' to be the operator of the machine. To reflect on our course it becomes evident the reverse is the case. The body and environment formed a mind of humanity. We see in all areas across the globe a reality where those with the most physical power reign. Men being stronger than women have always been favored; been dominant. A leading nation is one with the greatest wealth and weapons; or military prowess. Oppression was a successful means to control behavior because people feared physical power, most especially the police 'force'; to say nothing of the trauma an all powerful God could inflict. It is as though the deleterious natural events, as earthquakes, severe winds or floods; and predator-prey animal behavior encountered by our primitive ancestors; were so overwhelming; so disturbing to our psyche, that we retain a primordial fear of something 'out there' to this day.

So, we find ourselves with a natural arrangement favoring individual freedom, or SELF-discipline; but instead the environment is controlling the person. And we have what is considered the highest evolutionary product of Mother Earth, who not only doesn't accept the overall predatory natural actions, but is afraid of them. Overall direction of human progress is toward escape from oppressive behavior; from environmental harm. It is fair to deduct that not only are we not in our right mind; as for an organism to be compatible with its environment is a basic biological principle; neither do we seem to be in our right environment.

Another peculiarity is where the intrinsic structure of the physical world has a homeostatic arrangement capable of providing continuous existence; it holds an extrinsic negative direction that brings things to an end. Of even greater concern is where human art and poetry suggests aesthetic attachment to the normal state of nature; instead social structure remains attached to the extrinsic motion; most evident in the rise and fall pattern of people and nations. Of greatest significance and something worthy of serious consideration exists within the fact that when human consciousness was allowed to function in the same manner as the intrinsic structure of the physical body and environment; where energy was allowed to flow from the 'inside-out'; despite only a rudimentary beginning the REAL world, and REAL human potential rapidly began to come into view.

There are many celebrities throughout the human course. We can't dismiss the fact that the most reverence expressed went to the spiritual teachers. Where many oppressive religious and secular government systems rise to great heights, and then fall; the teachings of Buddha, Mohammed and Jesus drew a conscious connection with people that endured throughout all these linear changes. Spiritual practices of a culture, no matter how contrary to factual knowledge are slow to fade. Even today despite forty years of coercive direction of thought away from religion, to scientific truths and political social guidance; ancient beliefs and practices persist. Like the delusions of a psychotic individual are 'invisible' to others, but we can't bring the individual into our reality; so seems the mental state of religious fundamentalists. There seems little difference in the thought process of the Muslim, who straps a bomb onto his/her body, or the Christian who starts firing away at the abortion clinic; both killing innocent people. The likeness in the two individuals exists within mentality. Each holds an image of a God who thinks as he/she does; and expresses the primitive religious God with an oppressive mentality.

The similarity to the insane individual, who believes his/her delusional world is real, and can't be convinced otherwise; also becomes evident in the resistance of the human establishment to truths. Here though we can see a distinction between religious and secular establishments. Despite initial reluctance, secular establishments eventually realize the truth, and incorporate it. Although still into an oppressive system; thus maintaining the illusion it was their idea, strengthening the concept 'all comes down from above'. Where religious hierarchy, under the illusion ancient literal works are the actual words of God, and therefore inalienable and perfect; in actuality continues to exist separate from truth, stays within a world made by an ancient religious body; and distorts scientific knowledge in a manner compliant with that ancient mentality. There is an unspoken message delivered by all major religions relative to our sense of truth, love and fairness. This well could be the communication from God that is inalienable and perfect; not words from a human mentality; an ancient reality that has died, and needs to be buried.

What really matters in these illustrations exists in the fact that the delusions of psychotic individuals, even though they are invisible to others can be explained; in that it is a disturbance in the real-idea mechanism; the body machine. When bizarre ideation in these people surrounds an invisible God, it is possible to determine whether neurological chemical imbalance is the cause. We can also determine relativity of prior religious instruction to the ideation and deduct the degree of distortion. Where research has extracted knowledge relative to psychological pathology on an individual basis; the dissociation of the consciousness of humanity is essentially ignored. It seems just common sense that there is but one physical world; so there should be one consciousness of humanity; as there is one consciousness of inhabitants in each ecological setting. Not only is there one physical world separated in multiple conscious pieces; so is one God. Despite extremely strong emotional attachment by uncounted millions of people past and present to variable religious teachings; all relative to the one God, or one Spirit; the issue escapes ascertainment of truth. Throughout history there is nothing to compare with the emotional impact of personal relationship to God. It is as though oppressive and coercive means to unite the thought for/or against a religious view have failed; so we are just advised 'to never discuss religion'; to tolerate all beliefs. Thought moves the body. Our overall dominant thought has primitive roots. Failure to escape the primitive foundation of objective thought, we extend all energy toward physical analysis. Seemingly oblivious to the fact this mindset has not been our navigator; not what brought the knowledge into view. The dominant human emotional attachment has been to an 'invisible' God; and direction toward truth, comfort, compatibility and common welfare has flowed from common inherent social needs within 'invisible' personal consciousness.

With feet planted firmly on the ground, neither treatise of philosophy, nor a religious doctrine can form a logical deduction to provide accurate evidence of ethereal existence. It is so obvious that the primitive mind was not in contact with reality. The world they saw was an illusion. Truths began to arrive from within the personal consciousness of someone, often uneducated, and with low status on a professional hierarchy ladder. Still we abandon only the pieces of the primitive world proven incorrect by actual physical analysis. Ignore the nature of personal consciousness and human ideals because they are less tangible and defy physical definitions. We continue a fundamental primitive social structure, and to view things through a basic materialistic mentality, even though that too, has proven to be incompatible with the heart of the people. Through factual evidence, we understand the error in physical thought, but our pre-occupation with the physical world, may have credited the brain as the contributor of truths; when in fact 'personal consciousness' was the source. The mind acquired by the body of what is visible, has proven to be inaccurate, unstable and incompatible. It is astounding that as the introduction of technological marvels clearly reveals a human potential that most likely always existed, but was buried under an oppressive social reality; still no effort is extended to explore the human psyche in its entirety.

All indications are a 'person' is pure unlimited conscious energy. Personal consciousness is the life of the body; has been the life of our world. Each person has equal basic needs. By the time a human reaches adulthood, the 'person' may become deeply buried under an acquired mind. This may be to a degree where true personal needs, and identity only surface on sporadic occasions, and only as a vague abstract conscious sense. Because we have formed an entirely materialistic reality, a 'person' can only be defined as individual awareness of existence. A 'person' has no physical characteristics; not even gender. An intact 'person' exists in the sane and the insane; in the genius and the developmentally disabled. Talent is an equal possession of each person. Support for this equal existence should now be evident as women and minority groups have effectively demonstrated this 'personal' worth. There is no equality in expression, because of variable physiology, experience and a social structure inhibitory to its nurture and release. Enterprises flowing from within the 'person' are authentic, as are personal social exchanges. There is a common appreciation for this originality and sincerity. This suggests in addition to words and actions detectable by the physical senses; beneath social formalities; a pure conscious sense flows from 'person to person'; a 'common sense'. The strength of humanity flows from within 'personal character'. Herein is our only area of equality, but unfortunately is not equally nourished, or realized.

The Constitution of The United States of America is basically a means to satisfy 'personal' social needs. Each person has "inalienable rights"; has an "equal, but separate station—." Thomas Jefferson in our Declaration of Independence is talking about offenses to a common sense of 'fairness'. Intellectuals tend to consider the principles our country is based on, to be 'higher' ideals. "Life, liberty and the pursuit of happiness" are pieces of an inherent common mindset. These exist within each 'person', are not acquired by the brain from the environment. The only thing higher about these ideals is that they should be the foremost area; the central point from which all human endeavor emerges. To the mentality formed by a concept of time and distance, these ideals would be higher; on the top rung of the hierarchy ladder, because they have proven to be far more superior conscious entities than any concrete plan brought forth by mankind. Those people who followed these invisible beacons; these personal convictions, emerged victorious in all endeavors, and revolutions. Human ideals are what made the difference; what guided our ascent. This was understood by our founders. The recognition of which in essence began to return humanity to a state determined by "Nature and Nature's God." That we became prolific should not be an enigma. Our government was instrumental, in that the founders were relatively free from oppressive mentality. So, extended opportunity for the people to reverse the abnormal 'outside-in' mental formation by the 'most powerful', which traces to origin of primitive reality. They were not instrumental in forming a democracy, but in one arranged to defend a mindset of common ideals, as equality, truth, freedom, peace, compassion, personal worth and continuous life. These are inherent natural emotional needs. Entirely surround the manner in which a person inter-relates with the environment. Each person, no matter what shape the body is in, holds these expectations during daily encounters. At the end of the day, 'personal' happiness is determined by the manner of this pure conscious exchange during individual interactions. A state of justice is dependent on satisfaction of these needs by a government.

Personal dissatisfaction is relevant to only one event, which also seems an entirely conscious sense. Any action that overpowers a person will cause unhappiness, is an injustice. Whether initiated from a distance as a hurricane, or tyranny; or more immediate source as illness, or oppressive act from another person; a negative emotion will surface. Each 'person' holds an inherent respect for superior strength in another individual. The human predicament is one of inter-dependence. Our present state is such that each 'person' needs to become both student and teacher. Talents need to be shared. 'Personal' intellectual and physical strengths have been our rescuer from the primordial mental soup in which we were drowning. Strength differs from desire for 'personal power'. Strength helps, because of variable individual limitations; power control hurts, because it is inhibitory toward satisfaction of inherent conscious ideals, one of which is 'personal' need to nurture and express individual talent. At the end of the day 'personal' happiness is partly dependent on a sense of whether, or not we have done a 'good job', and that it was appreciated. When forced to labor in an area contrary to personal talent; or under rules inhibiting individual ability to be 'best that he/she can be; will cause unhappiness. As thought moves the body, this internal conflict can effect a negative response; in the form of either paralysis, or a physical confrontation. A sense of injustice is a personal conscious experience. Others may, or may not agree on whether a particular event was an injustice to either a person, or group. This natural circumstance may become especially evident through an overview of the setting in Colonial America.

The mindset of the Tory surrounded obedience to the King; considered justice to be a state determined by 'outside' rules sent down from above, and a hierarchy system of enforcement. The Native American assistance to the powerful and structured

British suggests their belief in 'outside' control as the way to correct the injustice inflicted by the white man. Trade was unfair; settlers kept moving deeper into the frontier, taking more of their land; there were sometimes brutal attacks by frontiersmen in retaliation to crimes committed by tribal outcasts. Native adaptation to this foreign reality flowed with the social structure most like their own tribal order; a hierarchy system, with status determined by individual degree of physical power; just like the appearance of the natural world. Tribal leaders gave support to the British, where a structured hierarchy system existed; where material gain appeared to flow toward those with the most physical power. In likeness to the steadfast laws in nature, subservience to the British system of laws may have appeared the way to material success.

A different mindset is expressed by the Whig. Here we see a support for personal worth, and allowance for self-discipline; a hatred of oppressive structure. The overall Whig attitude is relative to a common 'inner' sense of fairness; and an emerging intent to move the social world toward this 'personal' satisfaction. The method to achieve this end began by formation of a Continental Congress, who composed letters to King George III and Parliament requesting correction of the injustice. Quaker influence especially prolonged this approach toward a peaceful resolution. When this failed, the move toward justice was enacted in the same age-old oppressive manner. A loyal Tory farmer might find his property destroyed; a spy was tarred and feathered without a 'legal' trial. Where the Whig accurately claimed oppression as the source of discontent, they were oppressive to all, who did not conform to their way of thinking. Most especially to the Native Americans, who did not share their Christian beliefs. To overpower another person is always an injustice because it is contrary to a natural conscious desire for entities as equality, freedom of thought and compassion. The nature of justice was not; and is not understood; because the perception is not acquired from, and does not fit into the reality formed by mankind. The American Colonial Era still held a very oppressive mentality. Christians overpowered those considered heathens; the British, French and Spanish all fought each other; the Tory Party fought the Whigs; the Native Americans and the palefaces fought; and the Native American tribes fought each other. Human reality was; and still is a power struggle arena. An environmental place incompatible with a consciousness where a desire to love, and be loved is the most primary need.

There is much intellectual detail relative to historical events, but only one factor may be significant in consideration of our ascent; and herein our identity may become evident. Thought moves the body, and our ascension was relative to attitude changes. Not only was it attitude, but a guidance directed by intrinsic pure conscious ideals. In essence the transition was brought forth, as individuals moved from physical control, an oppressive mentality; to self-control, an ideal mentality. This occurrence began within western civilization. Tediously diffused throughout Europe, incited revolutions, overcame physical obstacles and culminated in The Constitution of The United States of America. The conscious change was from desire to have power over another person; to feeling a sense of responsibility for the welfare of another person. This change is comparable to the exemplification of Jesus, which most likely is the root; the one responsible factor in our direction toward release of personal potential. Personal awareness of existence, a sense of fairness, and choice to adhere to that sense may be the only area of human equality.

We can't dismiss the fact western civilization led 'the way'; and that 'the way' flowed from the inside-out; from the heart of the people. Change did not 'come down from above'. The establishment resisted truths. Those who introduced behavioral and physical truths suffered. Conscious evolution was not a spontaneous occurrence by any means. People who adhered to personal convictions endured hardships. Social reformers were punished; many died in revolutions. Innovative changes were preceded by personal sacrifice. To examine the 'brain' of the people who 'made a difference' would not explain what made them 'special'. Most likely the answer lies in the obvious fact each was free from the social, occupational, professional or religious mentality of his/her era. Where the majority of people are guided by a mind acquired from the 'outside', these innovators and reformers were in a natural state; where the 'person' directs the body; or true self-control. We respect these celebrities, but don't seem to recognize the nature of personal convictions. Perpetuate an educational system determined to fill minds, instead of nourishing and releasing the celebrity within. There may be no academic curriculum ever to enhance self-realization; to release this 'supernatural' person within each of us, as well as the lessons of Jesus that diffused throughout the western world. The story of Jesus had an emotional impact that began cohesion of personal consciousness with God, and with each other; and thus the collective western consciousness with God.

To determine whether this conscious cohesion is factual; whether indeed it was God, and not human intellect alone that 'led the way' toward comfort; we may have to do little more than consider the nature of truth. It should be obvious by now that the primitive reality based on the appearance of physical forms was inaccurate. There is more to reality than the objective world. Thoughts formed by physical appearances are often illusive. Progress in essence seems escape from erroneous thought; from collective thought formed by the appearance of things. The physical truths which brought more of our reality into view are not images of forms. Photosynthesis, gravity, atomic fusion, chemical bonds are not realizations acquired through the physical senses. Acquisition and comprehension of this knowledge is considered relative to a deeper intellectual capacity to analyze and reason. This knowledge too is relative to the objective world, and cerebral function; but what almost seems overlooked, is what matters most. The reality automatically formed by the body machine is not only partial, but is often illusive and incorrect. This is recognized, and effort has been extended to expand development of the deeper intellectual ability. Little consideration seems to be attributed as to why this is necessary; to the nature of this human endeavor. We seem to consider this intellectual quest relative to our physical superiority; to having the highest rung on the evolutionary ladder; but show no recognition of a human peculiarity in the overall predator-prey physical natural world.

To fit into the overall physical picture, and be compliant with basic principles of biological adaptation, our adaptive devices should have been adequate means to plug us into the natural world, and provide need satisfaction. Instead, conditions were so adverse to the human psyche that it seems to have become dormant. Psychological defense mechanisms and a pseudo-ego could have become adaptive mechanisms to protect the 'perfect self' from incompatible thoughts and behavior. The intermittent natural events that overpower the normal state and bring things to an end had the most profound negative emotional impact. These events could have evoked fear to such a severe degree that it caused personal paralysis. In awe of the detrimental effects when overpowered, a submission to physical supremacy ensued. Individuals became subservient to outside authority; and mankind to an outside 'supernatural' being, a god. A human mind then became formed from the outside in, which is a reverse circumstance to all other life forms, where direction flows from the inside out.

Another natural peculiarity that seems to escape consideration is the fact that this outer negative motion that brings things to an end does not fit into the overall picture of basic structure. The intrinsic structure of the physical environment and body is one where each entity has a talent; which it contributes to form a larger entity; and so on; with all parts contributing harmoniously to form the whole; a repetitive pattern enabling continuous existence. That this outer negative motion conflicts with basic structure, and has been so adverse to the human inhabitants, the highest evolutionary product, suggests it was not part of an original state. The human psyche desires everlasting life, and intrinsic physical structure is to provide just that.

The most important element in this analysis is that the entity bothered by this negative physical motion is the 'person'. As personal consciousness escapes scientific explanation, has no physical substance, defies academic definition and is adverse to physical conditions would suggest earth is not its Mother; not its origin. The brain is a machine part, so most likely this physical organ does not produce a non-physical pure conscious entity. It would seem personal consciousness could be acquired with the first breathe, as SELF has proven to be the life of the body,—and this is when the umbilical cord is cut, and a personal existence starts. Or more in accord with Biblical beliefs this life could trace to an original man, and somehow accompanies genetic transfers. Where personal consciousness comes from, and where it goes remains a mystery because we always think through our limited physical perspectives. To transmit thought is the brain's primary function, which does raise the possibility there is in addition to the objective world, a pure conscious dimension in our midst.

Further consideration may reveal this is our source, and the place to which our journey returns us.

We have already considered how real the delusional world is to the insane person; how difficult to reason with them, or bring them into our reality. Likewise, how the human establishment has always resisted truth, firmly believed its illusive world was real. The problem was that the foundation of the world created by the human establishment was built by the physical senses. The mentality so formed in essence became the looking glass from which thought was reflected. We continue to view things through this materialistic mirror. Everything takes on a material form. The reason for the delay in realization of physical truths is they are not reflected by that mirror. In essence the physical mind is a shield to the realization of truths. We have an intrinsic psychological need for truth, and therefore must have an environment and physiology capable of providing satisfaction. Truth may be right in our midst, but escape our realization because our vision is obstructed by a mentality that is wrong. Those who made a difference, who brought forth truths and innovations, obviously were not copying reflections of what already was known. The place the desire for truth exists, the place truths are realized, the place true vision occurs is within personal consciousness. The reason some perceptions are abstract, some entities escape definition, we can't reach agreement on the existence of God is most likely because our thought is reflected through a mind based on time and distance, on an inaccurate appearance of material forms and actions, and a primal fear of physical power. The psychological state of humanity may be comparable to physiological sleep. As a person gets swept into an illusive dream, so may the true self of humanity be dormant, while we are swept into an illusive reality, conform to the social establishment. Unfortunately here too, it seems an alarm is necessary to provoke awakening. Nothing seems to reveal true self-worth, our personal potential, and ability to feel a sense of responsibility for each other; than crisis and devastating events.

We also hold an intrinsic sense of lack and separation, always strive for more; but it can never be fulfilled through a mentality that by nature enslaves and limits. To carefully consider some almost intangible areas of progress, it could be construed the only thing we are lacking is truth. Because we have separate stations in body as to time and space, and harmful 'earthy' events are so contrary to conscious needs; we seem to have the mental fixation of being on our own. The same fixation seems projected to the physical world, as though planet earth is an isolated existence in a vast universe. Again this perception may prove faulty, be another reflection from the materialistic mental mirror. Our material fixation also holds the illusion we penetrated the physical world to find truths. These mental fixations in essence may be residual primitive states from when the body and environment formed and moved thought. The entity we actually penetrated to find truths was consciousness. A desire for truth, an idea of what the truth might be, and personal dedication preceded realization. We reached a greater conscious depth, found pieces of the real world within our thought. Our greatest achievement has been in the area of communication. All indications are our destination is a place called Reality; and the transit line that will take us there will be Conscious Unity. Our journey was not, and is not linear; nor was it planned by mankind. The primitive body machine may have formed a synthetic separate self in likeness to images of separate physical dimensions. We can't overlook our deepest conscious need is for love, and love knows no boundary. We begin to assemble the puzzle pieces that exist as scattered abstract perceptions within personal consciousness, and move toward a common place. That we are separate from each other and God may all be an illusion. We just need to stop believing the lie; the mind of physical images.

Each infant acquires a reality according to genetic inheritance, individual physiology and experience. The person becomes the center of, or holder of a reality. A common saying is that a person sees things through his/her own eyes. This seems true. A 'good' person sees the best in others; an honest person will tend to trust others; an artist will tend to view an object in a different perspective than a banker; and so on. A personal reality is relative to individual perspective, which is determined by mindset. We can see that there are also group mindsets. Each family, school, community, occupation, culture, political organization, profession, religion or nation will have a mindset of their own, and certain perspective. The individual and group mindsets, despite even extreme variation, all have a common similarity in that they are reflections of basic environmental appearance. Each human body has a real-idea mechanism, a brain and central nervous system that will automatically transmit an environmental image to a person. And each image will be of material forms that come and go; are temporary. The physical senses deliver an environmental image to the person, where vision then occurs. Pathology in this mechanism, as either blindness or deafness will limit a personal view; but not affect the basic mindset. As there is no difference now than in prehistoric times in this basic mechanism, in either body or environment; this materialistic view has formed an overall physical mindset, a collective mindset of mankind. This is the foundation, the governing mind through which each individual sees. In essence, this natural mechanism endows humanity with a basic common perspective, or an automatic application of form to thought. The individual and collective human consciousness thinks in forms, or structured thought. A dominant temporal materialistic mind frame determines vision, and confines us to an objective reality. To further consider the changes in the collective consciousness throughout our course, raises a suggestion our eventuality will be freedom of thought from this restrictive objective barrier.

In the same manner individual perspective changes during a lifetime, so has the collective perspective of humanity changed throughout its lifetime. Energy flows from the inside-out in all living things to form the whole; and so it has been with the consciousness of humanity. Gradual generational changes move us from a perspective acquired through a mind of images, which initially transformed all thought into a physical form; toward one acquired from a deeper vision within personal consciousness. The abandonment of mythical forms and gods, and a flat earth is all relative to a transition in vision from eyesight, to insight. Where the normal physiologic process is to transform thought into physical forms, we can see this ancient mind so formed was almost delusional, and placed our ancestors in an extremely incompatible world. The ancient perspective, acquired through the mind of physical images, formed a social reality in likeness to environmental appearance, where a hierarchy system was determined by physical power, or material wealth. Therefore aristocracy made the rules, making the reality most incompatible to the physically weaker, to the infirm and poor. To consider conditions today, we can observe changes in collective vision have been far more progressive in material matters, than in the human social affair. The best we've done is clear the physical view, while master-slave remains the basic social mechanism. There seems little change in the basic physical mindset. Changes remain within a primal physical perspective. The heuristic accuracy of past common sense observations is almost ignored. Instead of expanding this art, we insist on a scientific method of analysis and concrete evidence in all matters.

The collective consciousness of humanity expanded from a simple awareness of environmental appearance to actual comprehension of governing physical principles, or truths. Thought continues to be formed through the primal perspective acquired by physical appearance, despite the fact it is now known the mentality so formed was incorrect, and the reality so created by mankind incompatible to personal need satisfaction. We seem deluded by the appearance of progress. Attribute success to human intellect and a democratic format. Arrange academic and social curriculum in a manner conducive to release of personal worth. Where this formula for success has been identified, the nature of the main ingredient has not. To continue to view personal worth in material terms is a primitive retention. The best we've done is acknowledged the worth of intellect, but by no means to a degree where even it supersedes physical prowess, or financial status. We fail to recognize the worth of a person exists within character, and it is of equal value. Failure to nourish personal character renders the formula useless. There is nothing to release.

Nothing had an impact on personal perspective, and its effect on the collective consciousness to the degree of the major religious works. Historical records should be adequate evidence to support the stronghold of religions. Religious education of a child was a firm parental commitment. Mankind has always had a conscious connection with both a material world and a 'supernatural world'. Well-being in an 'afterlife' was a primary concern throughout the human course. The ideation traces to our beginnings, where evidence of 'supernatural' worship was found in cave dwellings. To reflect on our course suggests the overall objective of mankind is to reach this 'afterlife', this place called 'heaven'.

The conscious transition of mankind was from a view

delivered by the physical senses, to one that flowed out from within personal consciousness. Our current knowledge of physical principles, or environmental truths began as a personal conscious sense. Knowledge is acquired through both physical senses, and entirely personal conscious senses. Physical animation is an automatic process. Realization of truths requires personal effort. It is realistic to consider the reason truths and personal conscious senses remain abstract perceptions, is they are overshadowed by physical, or concrete mental reflections. This effect becomes intensified by the problem; it is the physical mind, with its oppressive fixation that rules mankind. The ruling mentality seems to be on a perpetual ego trip. Historical events repeatedly demonstrate the self-love of the human establishment. Whether this has caused blindness, or action is deliberate; there can be little question its objective is material gain. Most likely this is the reason the focus of our progress surrounds physical understanding, because here a product emerges, which can enhance ability to oppress, and increase the establishment's wealth and power. To put forth effort to understand a concept of personal worth, or matters of love and charity would definitely not be in their best interest.

Life is a conscious ascension; for the individual, and humanity. Personal consciousness is the life of the body; of our world. Love lifted our feet. This brought us together in thought. Self-confidence grew, and our primal fears eased. We rose a little higher with each truth that became known, and error discarded. Our perspective changed, and we began to search for a new world. Really began to soar when we entered a place called freedom. We became guided by ideas as equality, peace, compassion, personal worth, truth, freedom and everlasting life. As more and more people followed these invisible beacons, we moved toward a state of justice. Weapons were laid down, and slaves were freed. Equal rights were extended to minority groups and the sick were healed. We expanded educational opportunity and started welfare programs to help the poor. Automation and technology enhanced our ability to share thought. All moved toward protection from environmental harm, and the prolongation of life. We continued to gain altitude, our potential seemed unlimited. A United Nations was brought into existence through which this inner energy could flow from across the globe. This place of comfort called heaven was beginning to come into view.

This journey of western civilization was navigated by the heart of the people. It is a simulation of the life of their most revered celebrity. A change in perspective from an oppressive mentality, to a just mentality was the secret to success. Should it have been allowed to continue, we might have found what is considered spiritual and supernatural is in fact our true conscious nature. Human ideals have proven to be a natural inherent social conscience. Our ability to feel a sense of responsibility for another person is what identifies us. Human identity is not in body, but personal consciousness. Happiness is dependent on satisfaction of our sense of fairness; on our sense of equality, truth, freedom, peace and compassion. This is our humanity, a common sense, the only way to a compatible social reality; to heaven on earth.

The exemplification given by Jesus surrounds the Golden Rule; the manner one person treats another person; evokes our common sense of fairness. If not from God, then what explains the existence of this pure conscious sense? The New Testament of the Bible repeatedly warns us to avoid carnal influence. Humanity has been guided by an abstract sense of truth, not our concrete mentalities. The crucifixion of Jesus may be a symbolization intended for the whole of humanity. The message may be that death of the oppressive physical mentality, will bring us to life, and enable us to ascend. Because even the rudimentary release from oppression extended by the American founders has done just that!

The End Times

Where we seem to have acquired the notion we are biological products, with the complexity of our brain placing us in a position of hierarchy on an evolutionary ladder; consideration of the human course, and physiological structure of the environment; suggests this idea to be an illusion;—more sophisticated than other long abandoned thoughts, but still an inaccurate perception formed by appearance. The human course in essence seems an escape from the mind, and social realities formed by physiological adaptation. Those—who made a difference—, who navigated our course were not guided by the human establishment,—but by personal convictions. To adapt to the immediate physical and social environment is automatic; but realization of physical principles, behavioral truths and talent requires personal conscious effort.

It seems reasonable to assume as the energy from which our physical world emerged has no origin; came from nothing; so then should a reality be in existence where something can come from nothing. A world different than hours,—a world that had no origin,—came from nothing,—just is an ever-present existence! Such a world would then have a different consciousness as well, be a free flowing ever present energy.

That to our mind everything comes from some form of matter; with an intrinsic genetic arrangement to follow a certain course, and harmoniously blend in compliance with an overall scheme; that we can't even perceive a nothing; that our mind is constantly filled with thoughts about things; that we can only identify and utilize already existent principles, and seem to do little more than copy natural mechanisms; suggests we are not original, or natural offspring of such a free flowing consciousness,—of an ever-existent world without form.

To consider such an existence unlike our reality, would tend to eliminate the explanation of the person, or consciousness we call God, to be a greater intelligence,—a designer—as these are limited cerebral activities,—or physical function. Intelligence is a mental faculty produced by a brain. Likewise, the theory of evolution just seems applicable to changes in already existent physical forms. Our extrinsic mind formed by appearance of the material world connects us to temporal existence. Still from quantum mechanics we can almost conclude the physical world emerged from an ever-lasting existence without form. Where forms to the eye, appear separate, at the molecular level, we see this is not the case. Particles of a form are not separate from the environment. All seems part of one existence, in which change is only in appearance of forms. Basic principles are steadfast, or everlasting. To which certain conscious characteristics do connect us,—most especially the desire for everlasting life. Of even more significance than physical analysis, may be consideration of the manner we acquire truths. The nature of personal consciousness has not been identified. The 'invisible person' is not a physical substance. We can relate progress to transition from isolation, to civilization; then from oppression, to love; awareness of this capacity to love in western civilization traces to Jesus. After the principles of love were separated from religious control, and given to 'the people'; made a social allowance by the American Constitution; we began to soar. Suggesting as the physical world is in actuality one; so is human consciousness. When through our deepest feelings for each other; our capacity to love; we came together in thought; perception began to clear; the REAL world, and REAL human potential started to come into view. The answer to the enigma of life then may not be dependent on physical analysis; on cerebral mechanics alone; but cohesion of personal consciousness, of deepest thought; with each other,—and God. Our course shows this was the mechanism of our ascent.

Like the heart pumps blood, the lungs breathe or the stomach digests; the brain forms environmental images in a mind; which we can consider a physical mind, because the images are made by the body, and are of things. There is also a natural tendency to share thought, and to conform. Progress is relative to our ability to realize truth in the environment, as well as in human behavior and potential. Our so-called ascent is merely the correction and conformation of thought. Society adapts, and human reality changes.

Unlike other species, who know their behavior and environment, humans act like aliens. Still do not understand the nature of time, of temporal existence. Explore outer space as though to discover where we are. Have no understanding at all of personal consciousness, our most prized possession. Sometimes it seems like every five minutes, a new theory arrives, and reality changes. The human race certainly could be considered disoriented as to time, place and person; to not be in its right mind.

We can see on an individual basis, where a child is given the mind of its parents; likewise, throughout history, where a conquered people must adapt, or acquire the mind, or reality of the victor; and the variable social minds acquired from political or religious establishments. Can we consider any of these real, or a right mind, as they all begin and end, while the physical world of its biological attachment holds steadfast principles, do not begin or end? The human mind is really a very fragile, unstable entity formed by the more physically powerful, and almost forced on others. Is an ever changing entity, as specific areas of thought are corrected. So, possibly the foundation, or overall mentality; even the 'outside-in' manner of formation, could be incorrect as well. Account for the reason we search 'outside' the visible world for origin. Our pre-occupation with the visible world, the world perceived through the physical senses seems to have formed many erroneous realities; worlds that begin and end. So, perpetuation of that basic mentality formed by 'outside' objects, may have formed a religious and scientific existence premise that is wrong. Answer to the enigma of life may not exist 'out there', but within consideration of the nature of personal consciousness in relation to the theory that basic physical energy exists seemingly without a beginning.

It is not possible for something to come from nothing. Therefore, a reality should exist of a different nature, than ours based on a beginning and ending of things. As basic energy has not been, and of course can't be proven to have emerged from NOTHING, but just exists; suggests the physical world, and its inhabitants are within an everlasting place. A reality that has no beginning and no end, no physical form, or DNA arrangement; and therefore could hold a like consciousness;—a mind that is not formed by a body machine, and a world of forms; had no beginning, and will not end; is without form;—and in actuality, our world could somehow be an extension of that consciousness;

in which case that 'God', and the physical world could be the only part of existence we will ever be able to realize. A sort of imitation world could have been brought forth just for us. It is reasonable to consider God as the source of personal consciousness as it has no 'earthy' origin or composition. There is also the fact that intrinsic structure and planet earth in its natural state is compatible. The manner body mechanics automatically provide a reality could fall in line with this possibility. We can also see if we follow our hearts,—our deeper conscious awareness our reality moves toward truth and compatibility. Neither can we dismiss that the beginning of this insight and personal identity traces to Jesus, who is said to be the Son of God. The only thing we can be certain of is we are no longer in our original state. We clearly are in a 'world gone wrong',—and our mind went with it!

Still, as existence is in actuality a conscious experience, should we be part of the consciousness of God, then we could have far greater expectations than we now can even begin to imagine. Our predicament could be resolved simply by changing the way we think. We may find ourselves with a consciousness not limited to physical perceptions. Descendents of a consciousness capable of bringing a world of forms into an existence, where there were none. Suggestion seems to clearly be that the physical world and its inhabitants did not emerge from a THING. Not from anything in likeness to the intrinsic laws that produce the things within the physical world! That like in our case a thought, an idea precedes a creation; so could the physical world have entered existence. Different in that in this case for the physical world to be created; since physical science shows we did not come from anything capable of being perceived through the physical senses, or intellectual devices; the idea, and means to create a physical world would be unlike the idea, or mind acquired from, or formed by that physical world, which holds a creative ability confined to the discovery and use of physical principles within that creation. In other words the scientific knowledge we have may not have any significance beyond being a human intellectual comprehension of our world.

To speculate on the manner a consciousness could bring a material world into existence; we could consider the manner mankind does this within that world seems to differ from usual intellectual mechanics, in that strong personal devotion is always involved. We have been given the image of a God with human characteristics. To consider this God as a Creator then projects a picture of the way humans make and understand things. To consider a physical world made in such manner seems ridiculous. Further consideration however, shows that human innovations come from deep within personal thought. Where we function through the mind given to us by our predecessors, environmental truths and innovations toward comfort arrive from, and are realized at what seems a greater conscious depth. This would seem to be true consciousness, and is what brings forms into our existence.

We can also note that every idea, action and innovation moving us toward unity flows from this place within personal consciousness. What becomes evident in the consideration of our course is an individual ability to separate from the 'outside mind' given by those who existed before them. It was the people who followed personal convictions, who introduced behavioral and environmental truths, and innovations toward common welfare. The frontier penetrated by our ancestors was not linear, but exists deep within personal thought. When the American Liberty Bell rang, the process accelerated. Of interest is that as more people found personal freedom from the mind of the era, despite increase in diversity, we moved toward compatibility. Allowance for free personal expression promoted a natural affinity, or conscious conformity. Separation then could also be an illusion. We all could be pieces of one consciousness, but it is simply a free flowing energy, and God could be the source There is suggestion we are separate, but equal parts of one consciousness, which is simply an unlimited energy without form. This can be found in the ethereal nature of common human ideals, as well as other aspects of our conscious anatomy. In the nature of our overall direction, and consideration of what constitutes, and causes some humans to be celebrated by others. A physical mind is not consciousness, is not a living entity. But more like a picture album, or a movie. The energy of motion, the life of our body, of our world came from deep within personal thought,—from within personal consciousness.

To consider our intrinsic conscious desire for everlasting life alone, could only suggest our perception of reality is not accurate. That an organism be compatible with its environment is a basic biological principle. The human mind is never blank, always holds perceptions; and everlasting life is the most primal human emotional need. It would seem then, to the evolutionary theory that we emerged from a primal cell would have to support relativity of that cell to an ever-active, everlasting world. We can be certain that primal cell did not emerge spontaneously from nothing! All forms come from something already in existence. Human creations utilize physical principles, a knowledge already in existence; evolutionary change proceeds from an intrinsic arrangement already in existence. For the physical world to have emerged from one source, would suggest that one source came from nothing;—and that is a physical impossibility. Compliance with an overall arrangement demands further penetration. To find the source of; the manner the one source, the primal cell came 'to be'! Physical analysis can't take us beyond this cell. Still, there must be more! Our body, and physical universe is primarily space; there is no physical formula, or substance to personal consciousness,—or the energy we call 'life'. We understand physical animation, but the origin of the energy of LIFE is what matters. These areas that appear to be nothing,—in fact are exactly what allows us 'to be',—and thus herein may lie solution. To further consider our structure, we may also determine that we are not original, but synthetic additions to an everlasting world.

To our mind, dependent on physical body and reflection of objects; where everything comes from something; an existence composed of anything other than physical substance,—becomes inconceivable. Still, our factual existence, without substantial explanation, combined with current understanding of quantum mechanics seems to support the idea we emerged from something other than physical substance,—or to our limited physical mentality;—from nothing. Energy 'just is'. Unlike forms, does not begin and end. So too, a person seems simply an awareness of existence, an 'I Am'; a conscious energy; and so in actuality may also be everlasting. The body and physical mind composed of forms are dependent on what seems to have become a defective physiology. Because basic arrangement is for homeostasis, or everlasting existence, but now external events overpower the process, and bring things to an end. It is certain animation of the body ends, although we have never ascertained at what point death of the last cell might transpire.

The person in actuality is the life of the body, and this conscious energy, like the most elemental energy particles forming our world remains an enigma. Neither is our capacity to love, tendency to bond with others understood. When we reflect on loved ones, it is not their physical appearance, but their character that stays in our thought. The 'person', and 'love of a person' is something far deeper than appreciation of individual personality or intellectual expression; goes beyond attributes formed by 'the machine', the brain. This person remains even when brain function deteriorates, and intellectual interpretation and presentation is not accurate. So as character attributes and deeper 'personal bonds, or love' remain even when the 'machine' is not functioning properly; so may personal character be everlasting, or continue to exist after the machine stops,—not need the machine at all. Loving relationships could continue after physical death, because the bond exists deep within personal character. Pure consciousness, or the 'invisible person' holds no physical traits. Defies intellectual interpretation. Personal bonds often exist separate from reason and logic. Are not understood by others, who simply reach agreement a very deep personal connection exists. A connection called love, and there is every reason to believe this same occurrence can happen with the entity called God.

Our most intrinsic structure of physical environment, and human consciousness guides us to the concept we are part of an everlasting existence that is unlike our reality produced by physical formations. Also, to consider our emergence from nothing, or an entirely different reality, as spontaneous seems a natural impossibility; because our overall natural arrangement is for a REAL world of objects to appear in a mind; or a REAL-IDEA interchange. The overall scheme is for a material world to appear in consciousness; and this would not be brought forth spontaneously from a world without physical forms; because the physical world preceded human consciousness, and every rung on the evolutionary ladder involves structural physical change. In essence the physical world is our life-support machine; and our body is programmed by nature to form a physical mind. Human reality is formed by this real world of objects. Our world may be a simulation of a far greater conscious existence. A world where consciousness is free; where thought is not dependent on a physical machine. Unlike the human mind formed by objects, but like the abstract conscious sense of personal existence, and the nature of personal character we sense in others. Something deeper than personality, or intelligence; but only recognize through a sense of 'good or bad'. Scientific findings can only suggest there is more to reality, to existence than physical substance;—than the physical world. With quantum mechanics showing physical forms are not separate from the whole,—in opposition to the image of separation acquired through the physical senses;—then the concept we are separate from God, or the whole of reality most likely is also an illusion.

Perhaps we can't perceive a nothing, because there is no such thing. There is only everlasting existence, to which the physical realm may have been introduced by a conscious existence, because matter could only have spontaneously evolved from something physical. As in the case of humanity, an innovation,—an addition to our already existent world always is a conscious creation; so may our world have been brought into a realm not composed of evolving forms,—a different reality,—an everlasting conscious existence,—by what humanity has labeled a Creator. This also would comply with the REAL-IDEA scheme, in that as the physical environment preceded human consciousness,—an IDEA,—a consciousness should have been in existence to perceive it.; and that the only purpose of the physical world seems to be to appear in consciousness, to procreate body machines; and purpose of the body machine,—to provide conscious access to an already existent world.

The only thing physical findings show is that we came from nothing. As this is a physical impossibility, it can only direct our thought to a conclusion existence within the time-space realm is not all there is! That the overall temporal reality formed by primitive thought; a foundation perpetuated throughout all the eras is in fact an illusion. Like ancient civilizations had a reality based on immediate physical geographic perceptions; unaware of lands beyond the horizon; of a global earth; we now contemplate the nature of energy in outer space through quantum mechanics; with the same limited vision—the question of where does it end, and 'nothing' begin. Consider it curves round on itself like a global earth enhancing a perception of separation from reality. The future may show this concept as immature as the ancient fear of 'falling off the end of the earth'.

We focus on exploration of the physical world in search of identity, and find the energy that evolved to form a physical world from which humanity emerged,—essentially 'just is',—just exists. In the same manner, when I contemplate my existence,—I find only an awareness that 'I am',—that I exist. As the most basic unit of our natural environment seems only a particle of unlimited physical energy potential, so does each invisible person, or Self seem a unit of unlimited conscious energy potential. The quantum theory may have directed us to a world that has no beginning, and no end; and the same world seems to exist within personal consciousness, where Self is a constant,—a never changing entity, that views an ever-changing world,—the only perfect part of our anatomy,—always aware of existence,—young,—or old;—asleep,—or awake;—an ancient alchemist,—or 21st Century scientist;—no matter the time or place,—no matter what shape the body is in,—surroundings appear within personal consciousness;—and this intact perfect self is always seeking perfection,—frustrated by injustices of the physical and social environment, emits an energy, strengthening throughout all the eras; moving as though with intent to end actions that cause temporal existence, and reach a state of everlasting contentment,—of 'heaven on earth'!.

The most basic intrinsic element of the material world, and

human consciousness displays properties contrary to an extrinsic 'beginning and end' appearance, and mentality. The nature of personal consciousness, or Self,—is to perceive only in the present. You may be in a history class, or having a memory,—but you are doing it in the present. This could suggest the condition of past, present and future is not real, or certainly not an original state of humanity. Not only do we always perceive in the present moment,—but we hate to wait, want everything now. It is evident that our course has been directed toward an end of separation in time, place and person. This been enhanced through improved education, transportation, medical care and communication. The place we meet, or come together exists within thought. We only have personal conscious access to the present, and only when several people are present at the same time and place, can there be agreement as to the occurrence of a physical event, which still may not be entirely accurate because of variation in individual perceptive mechanics. Clearly separation as to time, place and person interferes with truth.

To consider the relativity of progress to personal insight, and that it was through this deeper vision we came together in thought, could support temporal existence is a human illusion, caused by conscious separation from each other, and God. The reason for progress is that a reality existed separate from our awareness. Physical principles are steadfast,—always existed,— just separate from our knowledge. We find the reality acquired through the physical senses was incorrect, and adjust as perceptions of environmental truths arrive from some place deep within personal thought. Through our ability to reason, to strain perceptions, we find truths. Where the variable minds formed by the physical senses conflict; truths bring us together in thought. Induced a sort of conscious cohesion, ended many separate realities, and seem to direct us to an ever present world of environmental truths,—and conscious creativity! We exist in a world where conscious and physical energy is always available for personal utilization. Failure to recognize and comply with this physical and behavioral law by the governing factions of humanity has been the restraint to the realization of personal worth, and the real world.

Indications are past, present and future is entirely a human predicament. The natural occurrence is for personal awareness of existence, of surroundings to be an on-going process. Events separated by points in time are not active. A memory is a picture of something no longer active; and a thought of a future event may be unfounded, is not an actual active real occurrence. The present is really when awareness of surroundings, of existence happens;—and that is always happening. Awareness of existence happens while we sleep,—as a dream; it happens to psychotic people in delusions;—and I, personally believe it will happen with physical death,—at which point the synthetic reality created by mankind is what will disappear. Personal consciousness, or awareness of existence is always happening;—and within this realization exists our identity. Contrary to what we are taught,— that the objective world, and social world created by mankind through the physical senses and intellectual prowess in its likeness is REAL—is our reality; this does not seem to be the case. The objective world, and social reality are ever changing entities. Truths, or physical principles are steadfast. Human IDEALS are an ever present part of human consciousness. Physical intellectual ability alters with age, or brain changes, as does personality according to either intrinsic chemical, or physiological changes, or extrinsic social effects. The person, the SELF and its needs for pure conscious entities as, equality, truth, peace or love is always present; determines the nature of emotional responses to thoughts of the past, present and future; and as with old age when brain function deteriorates,—although cerebral interpretation and expression fails,—feelings for loved ones, and things for which we have common psychological affinity, as babies, or pets, can be observed to also remain within personal consciousness. Personal consciousness,—the entity in which the physical world appears,—itself, is a constant,—an ever present existence of which uncounted billions of individual machines, or bodies have acquired a piece. This acquisition called a 'person' could well be an extension of an everlasting existence we call God.

The physical world moves according to natural principles; the social world moves toward satisfaction of common conscious IDEALS. Therefore, when we are told to get REAL, it should direct us not to the objective world delivered by the physical senses; but to the IDEAL world existing within personal consciousness. Because it is not the extrinsic changing appearance of the objective world, but the intrinsic natural principles that are ever present, and form a compatible homeostatic arrangement; and the place within personal consciousness that these truths arrived from; that move us,—in actuality guide us from harm caused by intermittent extrinsic deleterious motions. Likewise, as the social world formed by the body, or physical mind, has proved incompatible, and many of these worlds have disappeared; so, it would seem they were temporary illusions. Also, the process where a personal reality is formed by governing human powers seems an unnatural condition. Appears not only as an anomaly, but has proven to be unnecessary. This outside-in process of mental acquisition, is contrary to overall natural arrangement. In all of nature, knowledge of reality, and means to continued existence is realized through internal factors. Including humanity, where 'awareness' is a personal experience,—intensified through meditation; and it is from a conscious energy derived from this common 'inner world' called the 'human spirit', that has guided us toward truths and compatibility. All seems to suggest the 'beginning and end condition' of the objective world was not an original state: and within each person exists means to realize everlasting life.

There are growing psychological theories that death is a part of life, is inevitable;—must be accepted. Such a thought would seem part of the illusion, acquired from the objective world; where to the physical senses, the body loses animation, the energy we call 'life' escapes physical detection. Thought moves the body. The invisible person is the 'life' of the body. Within Self is a desire for everlasting life. The overall arrangement is for an environment to satisfy a need. Therefore, the REAL world should be everlasting,—be able to fulfill this most basic human emotional need! There are many speculations regarding the circumstance of death, but if truth is to be known, we can't ignore that the natural arrangement indeed does support the belief that 'self',—'deepest personal awareness of existence',—'pure personal consciousness', 'the invisible person',—is an everlasting entity. Within each invisible person, or Self can be found pure conscious ideals, as truth, freedom, equality, love or justice. Unlike everything else in the human mind, these thoughts are not acquired from the objective environment, or the social hierarchy system formed by mankind. These entirely subjective entities can't be interpreted by our intellectual apparatus, or communicated in the usual manner of physical instruction. Still, these words exemplify our humanity, the conscious energy lighting our way. As it is from this IDEAL world, within personal consciousness that a real ever present energy moves the individual, the physical and social world toward steadfast truths, comfort and compatibility; and as this ensued as vision was directed from the physical and social world through retreats, monasteries and personal meditation; it can't be dismissed that God, is a person,—an ever present consciousness we reach through our deepest feelings; to remove the human garments we can find a very REAL entity, that has guided our thought,—our so-called ascent! We seem to have dismissed our guide; believing we could reach the summit on our own. Are slipping rapidly, and need to grasp that ever-present conscious hand now; lest we end up like poor Sisyphus, spending eternity getting the ball to reach the summit of the hill; only to have it roll back down, and start all over.

To contemplate on this skyward journey of ours, we can see in essence our destination seems toward an end of the separation, and consequent variable realities caused by differences in the spheres of time, place and person. We tend to focus on the world perceived through the physical senses. Believe what we are told, credit 'outside' authority; but only when coercive laws were compatible with common ideals, existing deep in personal thought did we accelerate. Almost blinded by automation and technology, lose sight of where these marvels came from; and where they are taking us. From an 'ever-present' inner world of personal conscious talent, and a common subjective ideation; came objective changes. Personal consciousness moves toward ONENESS, tediously bringing many illusory realities to an end. The objective world, what we consider 'reality'; scientists claim to be an illusion. We seem to have things backwards. Not the objective world, but personal consciousness, the place 'things' appear, is what is REAL.

The Christian expectation relative to the 'end of the world', and the second coming of Jesus should not be dismissed, but deserves careful consideration. There is increasing disbelief among younger generations as to validity of the Biblical interpretations presented by the religious establishment. An individual adapts to the environment. The brain forms thought separate from any personal effort. Personal consciousness has a cohesive nature. Thought moves the body. Through anatomic mechanics of body and consciousness, an individual will conform to the already existent world of thought in any area. It could be possible then to consider isolated primitive individuals conformed, or copied the appearance of predatory animal behavior. The environmental image as acquired through the physical senses is one where those with the most physical power survive. The natural conscious tendency to conform decreased isolation and brought people together in groups. The more powerful became leaders and became the source of a local reality, as others adapted to their thought. Thought also, through natural mechanics becomes habitual. The practice of coercive thought formation continues to be deemed necessary by leaders of people. When authority directed vision to the Bible, minds were formed accordingly. Our history is one guided by transfers of authoritarian power. Awed by the intellectual prowess responsible for the technological marvels we so appreciate, power was transferred to academia. Control by the left cerebral hemisphere where physical function transpires has always been the primary area of conscious exercise. Our primary focus has always been on the objective world, making the enticement brought forth by scientists irresistible. A transfer of allegiance from a God, who defies verification through the scientific method of analysis; to the human intellect, which can accumulate and utilize factual information became a part of coercive mental formation. Resistance to faith in an invisible God, and demand for evidence by a generation where only thoughts relative to the visible physical world are included in an educational curriculum is a natural physical event. However, a step the religious feel brings us very close to the 'end times' in accord with Biblical prophecy. To strain the ancient mentality from the Biblical soup, and the concrete thought from the science textbook; it may become evident there is no conflict between the message of both groups. The error of both groups seems to exist in preoccupation with the objective world. Genesis suggests we are no longer in our original environment; scientists say all has deviated from norm. Revelations describes a horrendous end to the physical world; scientists sound the alarm about diminishing natural resources, and the horrors of nuclear war. Where scientists offer a far more rational explanation, than the religious, who expect 'every eye to see Jesus coming in the clouds'; to penetrate this thing we call reality, may instead find the 'believers in Jesus' closer to truth.

The reason answer to the question of origin remains obscure could be that truth is overshadowed by physical images, by primary exercise and reliance on a mentality formed by the body and environmental machine. Neither religious or scientific authority recognize the significance of the fact we view everything at a current point in time, and the place we see, feel and identify things is within personal consciousness; or even seem to consider that not physical animation, but this pure conscious energy has been the life of our world. We are so blinded by the primitive mentality of something being 'out there', fail to carefully consider the similarity of reality to a dream. Answer then to the enigma of life would seem to exist not in our physical, but conscious nature. We need to abandon the 'mind of images' and reach a greater conscious depth, in the same manner physicists have penetrated the physical world in the laboratory. As there the appearance of 'things', or what we have considered to be 'reality', has proved to be an illusion; so would the foundation of the mentality formed by the illusion be incorrect. Where we have discarded pieces of this synthetic reality as steadfast physical truths arrive; we remain limited to think within the basic premise of separation and temporality. The teachings of Jesus move us to another world, a common place deep within personal thought; and physicists confirm the images that have always governed human thought are incorrect. All indications are the 'end times' will not be a physical, but a conscious event. In likeness to the age old belief, physical death releases the person, who will meet God; the same may be true for humanity. The only thing that began, and will end in the whole of existence may be the human illusion we call reality. A conscious unity through a deeper vision seems our direction. When we are one in deepest consciousness with each other and God the physical illusion may end just like awakening from a dream

The Christian religious establishment teaches that the Bible is the word of God. An omnipresent God, whose word therefore would not change with time. So, they perpetuate a 2000 year old mentality. Continue with an omnipotent God as ultimate ruler. Maintain a human chain of command. These authorities have made so many decisions as to what should be presented in the Bible, and adopted so much from other religions that it is fair to question its authenticity. Evidence that the Bible does hold the word of a God of love, as introduced by Christ, is certainly not discernable from literal interpretation. An oppressive mentality with clear acceptance of slavery, and inequality of women radiates from especially the Old Testament. The teaching tends to separate people, and reflect a somewhat selfish attitude in the individual, and the establishment. It would seem the eastern religions better parallel the example of Christ. It seems more compatible to consider the idea we find God not in what is visible, but in the invisible; and not in the 'way of the world' established by mankind, but within the heart,—the SELF.

To logical reasoning the idea of this ancient human mentality being the 'image' of an omnipotent, omnipresent, omniscient God of LOVE becomes almost absurd. However there must be some reason Jesus was the greatest celebrity of all time; that with the Bible as navigator, western civilization showed the way; that scientific discovery coincides with basic Biblical premise. The reason may be related to the fact the lessons were not intellectually sound, in fact described events contrary to physical possibility; still were compatible to the heart. The Bible had an emotional impact. Reached a common place deep within personal thought.

What is omnipresent in our reality is personal consciousness. A human 'receiver of perceptions', an awareness of existence is no different now than it was thousands of years ago; is an equal possession; and exists here, there and everywhere. This is not true of personality and mind, or physical thought. These are not the same now, as then; and not the same here, as there. Also, awareness always happens in the 'present', so by nature consciousness is ever present.

Omniscience also seems a trait of personal consciousness. All truths arrived from a place deep within personal thought. As did human inventions flow from this source. Personal success is an art, can't be instructed, or reproduced. Seems the source of 'good' decisions. Those which promote actions compatible to contentment of the individual, and others.

We can also consider omnipotence as a trait of personal consciousness. All determining battles were won not by the more physically powerful, but by the believers in common ideals. Words as equality, truth, freedom, peace, love, talent, everlasting life showed the way. These ideas exist only within personal consciousness. Are not derived from anything in the physical world. Pursuit has been for personal happiness,—or a state of justice; an entirely conscious experience.

Because of our preoccupation with the physical world, we demand facts, seek physical evidence to explain our origin.

Religious and academic authority continues to see a God with human characteristics,—with a limited human mentality. Careful consideration reveals not only is this not the case, but neither are people primarily products of physical evolution,—and neither is the physical world, the objective world as we believed it to be. Physicists have determined the foundation of our mentality; the primitive reality based on appearance of separate solid objects is an illusion. Therefore the idea we had a beginning, and will come to an end, in likeness to the course all objects appear to follow; is likewise an illusion. Making the facts, the physical evidence we so revere, also only relative to human intellectualization of the inner structure of appearances in our illusion. Combined with the consideration intellectualism was not made possible by physical sensory devices; not by visions acquired through eyesight, but personal insight; arrived from, and is realized at a greater conscious depth; a place within personal consciousness; and that also from this same source came the utilization of the knowledge so acquired; toward the introduction of manmade objects, as automation and technology, into our world; and acceleration of these objective changes transpired as personal consciousness was not only directed away from, but allowed freedom from thought formed by the illusion; when focus moved from human authority, to allow personal proximity to God, and respect was for this equal opportunity; to the extent it became a coercive conformity through American laws to defend personal rights; that then, a compatible diversity of talent emerged; supports that the idea 'all comes down from above' is an illusion; that within each human mind acquired from the illusion, exists an 'intact perfect self'; with a natural propensity to contribute a talent toward common welfare; in the same manner each cell of the body and environment harmoniously contributes toward the welfare of the whole. As objects are illusory, then the idea we are objects, or human bodies, and that we came from an objective source; would not be correct. Then, this would leave only an entirely subjective entity as explanation. We can further strengthen this thought with the fact our ascension was of a completely subjective nature.

All seems to suggest the ONE source we search for is not a thing, and would not have any of the traits 'things' have; as the physical sensory mechanism can only deliver images of 'things', then to these limited perceptual mechanics; a pure conscious existence, having no physical composition, could not be detected. Still, personal consciousness IS awareness of existence, and through which a deeper reasoning capacity brought us to the realization of behavioral and environmental truths; has been the prolific entity in our world. So, can we reason the Truth; the ONE SOURCE; the energy through which all is inter-related; the dream, and the dreamer; could well be the consciousness of God; if scientists find our objective reality to be an illusion, then disorder is in human perception; with the explanation for the perceptual disorder, and the uncounted millions of variable personal illusions; being dissociation of the one consciousness of God and humanity.

What physical evidence acquired through the scientific method has made clear; is a most definite awareness that things are not as they appear. The irony is physical evidence has incited antipathy toward traditional religious practice, because of the fallacy in literal interpretation, and most especially a history of religious oppression; compounded by revelations of the delusive image of God being the moral source of a religious order; while immorality within that hierarchy system has been exposed; while favoring the secular establishment, despite the same history. As well as an overall transfer of faith from God, to the authority of scientific communities; while deeper inspection of the accumulated knowledge, can only support the guidance given by Jesus was perfect, or exactly in accord with a natural order.

The era in which Jesus appeared held an extremely predatory mentality. An individual mind was formed by the 'outside', by human religious and secular authority. Jesus moved thought from objective sources, to a place deep within personal consciousness. Contrary to conditioned obedience to authority, guided people toward personal ability to reason. Gave no concrete explanations, or instructions. Taught in parables. The message was entirely subjective. Like in all living things the energy flowed from the inside-out. From a carpenter walking around the countryside talking to people, diffused a personal ability to reason. With it came a natural social conscience, a morality. An entirely subjective entity described in words as equality, truth, freedom, love, personal worth and justice. The thoughts formed an energy called the human 'spirit', which tediously moved social behavior toward satisfaction of these entirely subjective ideals. Our course and structure suggest it is the 'illusion' we call reality which will disappear, and 'mentality' exemplified by Jesus that will return. The precedent to progress was a social focus on personal character maturation, through meditation. This effected a change in thought; an escape from the physical mind acquired from the environment; to expression of a conscious energy from within. From an ever-present 'inner world', we find means to end an incompatible reality. From a common subjective ideation,— came objective changes.

Most likely, the same is true of the objective world in its entirety. All indicates it was consciousness that brought the physical world into an already existent unlimited everlasting reality. Just as a real physical world and human potential existed separate from the awareness of our ancestors; so still does the whole of reality await our realization. To consider the nature of our ascent, it becomes apparent the illusory world of the past was effected by reliance on a mind formed by the body machine; and the perceptual defect was corrected when vision began to flow from within personal consciousness; as personal maturations happened, a natural cohesion of deepest thought brought physical and behavioral truths into view; we became more coherent,—or, 'in touch' with reality.

That there is no physical explanation to describe personal consciousness; and that the unreal world existed when we were separated from each other, and God; and the real world, or truths came into view as we 'came together in thought'; could suggest our consciousness, in the same manner our body is dependent on satisfaction of physical needs,—is dependent on unity with physical elements; so is accurate conscious perception dependent on unity with each other and God. I do not believe there can be a conflict of subjectivism and objectivism in the consideration of either human origin, or reality. Physical objects come from principles already in existence. This objective world exists within human consciousness. As physicists consider it an illusion, it's almost like we share the same dream about things. The dream is formed by the body and environmental machine, which perceives images and thoughts. It is not the animated machine, but the receiver of those perceptions,—personal consciousness that has been the life of the machine,—of our world. Not our body, but consciousness has been the living growing entity, and this is not because of the body, but a personal capacity to reason,—to penetrate the appearance of the objective world. All suggests we are primarily conscious entities, but we are not original; require an objective view to form our reality.

Our direction was not planned by mankind. Quite the opposite. Truths, innovations and direction toward unity flowed out from the hearts of the people,—from within personal consciousness. Were resisted by the 'establishment', eventually accepted,—and then became incorporated into the oppressive leadership mentality that has always prevailed. The frontier our ancestors penetrated was not linear, but exists deep within personal thought. Conscious and physical energy is always available for personal utilization. Provided we comply with natural physical and behavioral laws! Physical principles do not change,—and the 'heart' of humanity,—the need for justice does not change,—and overall directional change moves toward compliance with these everlasting natural laws.

We need to strain the mental soup for truths. The basic foundation of our mentality is based on an illusion. There is only an ever-present world. The idea of past, present and future; of beginnings and ends;—of separation is inaccurate. Basic energy is always present; the physical body and environment has an intrinsic arrangement for homeostasis, or to be always present; and most of all personal awareness happens only in the present moment. You may be in a history class acquiring knowledge about the past,—but you are doing it,—are in the present. Where you hold a mentality of past, present and future—you only exist in a present state, suggesting we are part of an ever present conscious world. The place a world that begins and ends exists may only be in human minds, an idea derived from the appearance of changing forms. All indications are what will come to an end is an erroneous and oppressive mentality.

The Celebrity

Each of us arrives on planet earth with a wide-open consciousness. Enter an abyss called the future. Most get carried away by the current; rise and fall. For others, some invisible beacon seems to show the way. They begin an incredible ascent. Soar toward what seems will be unlimited actualities!
With feet planted firmly on the ground, we look up to these people. Encourage our children to follow. In time gravity eases. We begin to levitate. The hall of fame grows. These celebrities survive the element of time. Become everlasting. Their contributions and fame survive throughout all the eras. It may be of great importance to note the most respected celebrities have not been the scientists, statesmen, athletes, artists, entertainers or explorers; not those who introduced awesome physical accomplishments. The most outstanding admiration expressed; the greatest applause went to Buddha, Christ and Mohammed. The affinity for these spiritual leaders supports the idea we are more than physical forms. It becomes evident that although we are separated physically, within deepest personal thought we are equal. Share a vision; perhaps a vestigial memory of a compatible world. We remember a place of everlasting life; of personal

satisfaction; of justice. Thought moves,—is the life of the body. All arrangement of the physical environment is to support the body, which holds a primary function; to deliver images to personal consciousness. We are primarily conscious beings! Consciousness is our most prized possession. Not our body; but consciousness moves us; enables our ascent!

The journey on which we embarked was contrary to usual human endeavors. It was not planned. The means and destinations were unknown. Not only was not guided by human authority; but departures were delayed by governing establishments. Travelers ridiculed, and dismissed from academic associations. Those who introduced behavioral truths; inspired social changes were especially despised by governments. One— who had an emotional impact on the world like no other—was crucified; followers persecuted; and later social reformers faced firing squads. Surmounting all physical obstacles, truths prevailed. From these truths, radiates another unphysical characteristic. The idea and the innovator become everlasting. Their contributions become steadfast components, building blocks in an ever-changing human reality. Many of these people, who moved us forward, had very little, or no formal education! There is one thing all our celebrities have in common. Each separated from the mind formed by body and environmental instruction, and pursued a personal conviction. An incredible ascension transpired over the past two centuries, but the manner remains a mystery.

The celebrity is asked for guidance; for the formula to success. Jesus told us the secret is 'to love one another'. Other celebrities tell us similar indiscrete things like personal dedication to fulfillment of a 'dream'. Perseverance is the most common word used in regards to what made it materialize. All celebrities tend to credit other people for helping them along the way. Unlike other knowledge, there seems no means of physical instruction. Only the accomplishment and material rewards promote our awareness of these personal strengths. We try to extend the process through 'higher' education; make physical academic credentials the means to material gain. This may have benefited only a precious few. Overall this leads to a robotic conformity. Like all 'outside-in', or coercive methods, we find this may actually have disguised many personal 'dreams', and buried talents. We suspected cerebral exercise the need, but it seems the vision is within, brilliancy is personal consciousness, and faith is the means of making the idea materialize. The reason America became prolific seems clearly relative to a transfer of belief in the Divine Right of Kings; to the Divine Right of EACH PERSON;—to a belief in personal worth! Our rapid ascent suggests each person is unique, a precious talent on which the whole of humanity is dependent. American success happened when outer structure was arranged to direct vision to an inner awareness.

A child's primary education surrounded something in existence beyond the view delivered by the physical senses. Obedience was to Love, and a Golden Rule. Religious works were expected to help the traveler reach a destination of everlasting contentment. For the majority in America, the Bible was the guide. The words incited a deeper realization, had an emotional impact. An unspoken message radiated from the parables of Jesus, a sense of fairness, and being loved. A growing sense of personal worth could have been the source of our success. We developed faith in ourselves, began to follow our conscience, rather than the oppressive way of the world. Separate from the words, a conscious sense told us we have nothing to fear, are not lacking in anything. Our intellectual expansion was preceded by a maturation of personal character. We began to find identity, our sense of fairness and ability within. This was not promoted by secular leaders, or planned by them. The only conformity relative to this emerging conscious strength seemed to exist within the 'heart' of the people. From here came encouragement of personal prayer to a God of Love; and obedience to this inner guidance. Children who did not 'play fair' were sent to their room to 'think' about what they've done. The family focus on obedience to this inner vision was extended through public education. Emphasis seemed constantly to be on 'becoming a better person'. The children understood, and obeyed. Soon, a compatible diversity of talent emerged.

The accomplishments of these children steadily increased in magnitude, and brought forth a dramatic change in our social reality. Previously unseen physical principles were introduced to our world, and these revealed our engineering dexterity. Behavioral principles became common knowledge, evident in a growing sense of responsibility for the welfare of another person. The frontier they penetrated was not linear, but exists deep within personal thought. The world they brought into existence was almost a complete contrast to the place that existed before them. As every thought in the human mind has a real source, this would seem to suggest we can acquire information from more than the visible world. The knowledge always was right in our midst, we just were not aware of its presence. The only place knowledge exists is within a consciousness. All the prayers may not have been in vain, but answered for the welfare of humanity.

Love was the motivator, radiated out from family to community and nation. The deeper conscious awareness that has always been aroused by spiritual teachers, works of art and ceremony gained social proximity. All seems to indicate a 'person' is not primarily a physical body, but a pure unlimited conscious being. Our meeting place was within personal consciousness.

This is where our knowledge was found, and where it is shared. The place where the knowledge is utilized, and where the contributions are appreciated exists deep within our thought. The manner we expanded our reality, and moved toward comfort and compatibility was not directed by human authority. The 'establishment' still doesn't even comprehend it, is not able to give any concrete explanation.

We may have failed to recognize personal character as our source of strength. As material thought always remained dominant, we may have been deceived; again swept into the illusion 'all comes down from above'. Power was transferred to academia. Where to organize, enhance intellectual exercise and share the knowledge seems in accord with a natural order; to idolize this ability may not be. We became dissociated from God. The 'people' allowed God to be dismissed from education, the media and all social affairs. Only gave God permission to attend religious services and events. We were advised to never discuss God, and obeyed for fear of losing friends. The energy enabling our conscious transition did not come down from above, but flowed out from the heart of a people who prayed to a God of Love. This was a free-flowing energy, and unlike things within the physical realm, can't be controlled, or reproduced; just needs to be released. Our phenomenal ascent could suggest not only are we primarily conscious beings, but our world is within the consciousness of God; of course in a manner difficult for our current time, space material oriented minds to even imagine.

The reason for our ascent was a knowledge; an ability to perceive it; and a common destination exist beyond the immediate separate physical realities, and behavior formed by automatic functions of body mechanics. The place we journey toward,—is truth; the means,—is to come together in deepest thought! In actuality we did not go anywhere; did not discover anything;—just began to realize a knowledge that was always in existence. The means was through personal escapes from the mind formed by the physical senses; in essence, transfer of thought from what was learned in the past, to the present moment. All knowledge arrives when we clear our minds, which is actually to rid it of past debris; and open it to allow ever-present truths in. Our primary human predicament seems that we live in the past and future, which is not real. Our celebrities are those who entered the real world; an ever-present place, where truths and personal talent thrive. Physical principles and personal talent were always in existence, just separate from our awareness. Personal ability to perceive this knowledge was always in existence. Celebrities may merely be expressions of what remains occult; our true common conscious nature, the means to secure a satisfactory reality for the person, and humanity. To reflect on our course may reveal the physical mind and ego is not only synthetic; but the root of conflict and unhappiness. There may be no better nomenclature than "human being" to describe our identity. The "human" is the physical machine; which through body mechanics forms a mind. The "being" separated from the physical images it holds is pure unlimited conscious energy; simply an awareness of existence; true personal consciousness, or SELF. Each person from birth automatically acquires a physical mind through adaptation to the immediate physical environment. This mind simulates environmental activity. The images perceived by primitive humanity were of predator-prey animal activity; motions as earthquakes, volcanic eruptions or floods that overpower the normal state and cause devastation. Views and thoughts were isolated; but still all ancient civilizations seem to simulate the environmental pattern. All became master-slave affairs; with intermittent wars that overpower and bring things to an end. Our progress is not relative to expansion of that primitive mind; but to its abandonment. Awed by the material gifts from our predecessors, we attempt to accelerate the climb through development of the intellectual machine. Make academic credentials vital to social survival. This approach may not only be inadequate;—but could prove detrimental.

Expansion of the practice of personal meditation;—of prayer to a God of love—was a precedent to progress. This suggests the natural mechanism to success exists within personal consciousness;—and that as the body is a machine that delivers perceptions to the Self,—and progress was not initiated by, but inhibited by the human establishment;—that the body machine well may be able to access a deeper conscious realm of existence;—that is unlike the physical reality; but an unlimited natural resource of creativity. To view the physical world, and copy actions is an automatic body function; but to realize a deeper dimension requires personal effort, and is something that can't be simulated, but expresses pure spontaneity. Where automatic adaptation is natural, it holds intermittent deleterious activity, an incompatible arrangement of inequality, where competition for physical power causes suffering. That an organism be compatible with its environment is a basic biological principle. It is the quest for power that causes harm to each other, and the environment. For an organism to flourish is dependent on the environment's ability to provide need satisfaction. We have a basic desire for happiness, which is dependent on physical and emotional need satisfaction. The only environmental condition interfering with need satisfaction is the motion in the physical and social environment that overpowers an organism, inhibits growth, and has potential to bring things to an end. That the intrinsic structure of the physical environment, and our thought is compatible; along with consideration of how automatic biological mechanics, provide need satisfaction, would suggest an original human environment where conditions that overpower did not exist. To further reflect on the human course, it becomes evident within personal consciousness is the means to restore that state. All progress is toward escape from environmental and social conditions that overpower, and cause harm. So, it would seem focus should be on personal character and talent; to restore its function as generator of the intellectual machine.

No person was more revered in western civilization, or had a greater impact on personal consciousness and behavioral guidance than Jesus. All events surrounding the existence, and followers of Jesus support the belief of the Christian establishment, that He was not only more than a human machine;—but more than a human being. The body machine automatically adapts to the environment; conforms to social circumstance. Becomes either predator, or prey; with variation only evident in degree of social acceptance. Christ interrupted that biological program. Through personal example and parables, Jesus diverted vision to another common environment; not a physical, but a conscious place. His lessons and instructions penetrated personal thought, conflicted with religious and social laws. Jesus taught our strength is not in body, but conscious connection with God; which He exemplified through miraculous events, where the 'believer' experienced changes contrary to physical laws. People followed His example to their death; contrary to physiological survival devices. Where Jesus may have introduced our REAL world and nature; given us identity of place and person; we continue to consider an extraordinary occurrence a 'miracle', and personal experiences with God, as 'mystical'. Keep our feet planted firmly on the ground. We followed, but restrained by physical thought, may remain unaware of the real message.

We describe "spiritual" experiences, as though this were

something almost abnormal; remain in either awe or disbelief, of what may not be "supernatural" at all,—but our true nature! Just like then, the world was not as it appeared, was not flat; neither are people as they appeared; are not masters or slaves. Our course shouts loud and clear that nature did not arrange for one human to be master, or overpower another; as this is the source of all conflict and inhibition of talent. Human oppressive mentality is the reason rebellion, war, starvation and suffering continues. Every master uses coercive measures, which are not conducive to either release of individual ingenuity, or contentment. Nor does it seem nature intended for any person to be a slave. There is an inherent need for freedom, and destination seems toward its fulfillment. Jesus was the 'spiritual' leader of western civilization. He never exerted power over anyone, did not coerce; just talked to people. Words produce a vision within self. The Bible essentially seems to say that God will protect us. A predator can't survive if there is no prey! This seems a natural solution, to end predation. Our vision improved, but remains inadequate. The best we've done is decrease the degree of bondage, and cruelty in punishment for disobedience. To give some in depth consideration to the nature of our course; and to decipher the Bible; we may find correlation with scientific findings. Consider that Jesus knew just what He was doing; indeed was more than a man. The Holy Spirit may not be mystical, but the true conscious energy that has been the navigator of our skyward journey!

To analyze the concept 'Christ was without sin';—we can see there is one thing Christ definitely was without—and that was the physical mind of His era!! And the most distinct message of the apostles is to not let the body, the environment control you! To leave all things, even your family, and follow the guidance of Jesus. We begin to acquire the mind, or thoughts of our family from birth. It is an automatic process, as is to acquire the mind of our peers and teachers as we age. To follow Jesus though was different, required a personal vision. There was nothing exact, all was subjective. The 'light' they followed seemed an invisible beacon, and guided them through places like equality, peace and freedom. The paths they were to follow were called truth and love; with justice being the eventuality. Discussion on 'the way' surrounded personal ability to move mountains; about coming to life, that "God is not the God of the dead, but of the living." No other taught like Jesus, in that the message was to free your self from the mind of the past and future, and enter the present. The place where appreciation of everlasting life, and an abundance of love can happen is deep within personal thought. To understand the message of Jesus is an entirely personal experience. So, in essence this message could move an individual from physical awareness, to SELF awareness. The body by nature is arranged to deliver perceptions to personal consciousness,—to the SELF! In essence, Jesus directed us to a natural state; to the place where real vision occurs. The physical mind is connected and limited to physical images; where SELF-expression, ideas that flow from deep within, are unique, authentic and have been the everlasting life in our world. Transfer of thought from physical control by the environment, to Self-realization through personal reflection and meditation; delivers the freedom we crave.

This personal freedom is the need, the answer to all our problems. Should each person become free from physical restraint, all else would fall in place. Personal vision is the only thing we lack. We can see just a rudimentary introduction of this SELF-worth moved us quickly toward satisfaction of physical and emotional needs; away from environmental harm. We still don't understand it all, remain almost blind, our vision clouded by physical thoughts. Freedom is an entirely personal conscious perception, and need. The only freedom possible exists within personal consciousness. We search for physical truths in the science lab, but this will never confirm personal identity. A person is a pure conscious entity, so contemplation is the only guide to this truth. Once realized, in essence the person becomes free from a false identity and reality.

The consideration that the American government gave freedom to the people is misleading. Democratic formats existed before, so alone can't be an explanation. To consider the people free from government power is another illusion. Aristocracy has always had the power, controlled people. This did not change, although tediously 'the people' did weaken that barrier. Thought moves the body. Our founders were free from an oppressive leadership mentality. They represented a people, who were free; not encapsulated by religious or secular government authority. So in essence, the people were already free, and the only logical source of that freedom is God.

Personal identity does not come from parents, government, religion, scientists, teachers or any other human authority; but from within. We look to these 'outside' sources, because of our training. Our physical mind is not free, but connected to these authorities. There is no physical freedom. Everything is interrelated. The same is true with our reality, because it was formed by a physical body and environment. This idea of freedom is very real, and has been a primary motivator. Our country began with a Declaration of Independence, and the sound of the American Liberty Bell has never silenced. Freedom has relatives, words as equality, truth, love, peace, life and justice. The Constitution of The United States of America was brought into existence by this common ideology, which continues to radiate from every step of social progress.

Words evoke an image within thought. Words as freedom, truth, love or justice have no form, or physical identity. The ideology our country is founded on has no physical substance, is a pure conscious sense, comprise personal needs of social exchange. To exercise this inherent social conscience is a personal art; and so was our ascent! The common denominator during our ascension was a personal belief in God, and an ideology which traces to a behavior exemplified by Jesus. We were told God is love, and were expected to obey God's law, which was to 'love one another'.

Why do we not consider the need for personal talent fulfillment; for truth and justice; for worldwide unity;—natural? Why do we not realize that within each person is a "natural" need for, and capacity to "love"? Why do we fail to realize our identity? Despite the abandonment of uncounted myths, and direction toward truth; we fail to agree the mind, and individual ego formed mechanically through physical adaptation is synthetic; incompatible with common inherent personal needs,—and according to ecologists, with needs of the physical environment. The mind of images, and resultant power control mentality is evil,—in that it holds not truths, but illusions,—and causes harm. The mentality has primitive roots, was brought into existence in essence by environmental appearance. Tediously changed by people with a deeper vision, but always remained within its foundation on time and distance; and a lack of something, or a need for more, a pursuit to find it 'out there'. True progress would be continued direction to escape from the illusory reality the mentality formed. Instead, maybe exhausted by production of a vast intellectual social machine; we return to sleep. Become submissive to the illusion personal well-being is secured through obedience to only human authority, again become enslaved; just in a more refined, or sophisticated setting.

We seem oblivious to the fact that the body and environment, which forms this oppressive mentality is said to be in a state of descent. There is no longer the perfect human, gas or oak tree. Everything has deviated from norm. This environmental mind also tends to simulate the body in that it initially grows rapidly, reaches a peak; then levels off, starts to decline, then comes to an end; evident on an individual, group or national level. We can see the rise and fall pattern throughout history, and certainly notice it in personal lives as well. This mind gets us nowhere; and it is again gaining a stronghold. Were this mechanical ability all there is to human consciousness, there would have been no ascent. When eyes are glued to the objective world, we follow the 'beginning and ending' course of physical forms.

The mind that determined our course was not of objects already existent within our immediate reality; not the mind that can memorize, repeat and copy what is visible. Today we have become so linear, seem to suspect the human brain is the 'person'; is what made our world a better place. The brain is an organic machine, as is the central nervous system. This machine makes it possible for the person to communicate with the environment. Messages are transmitted to, and from the invisible person, the self. Some perceptions are concrete, others are abstract. We perceive not only images of objects, and thoughts from others through words; but almost ignored are the perceptions that matter more than anything. There are entirely subjective transmissions as well; and these are what give us strength, move us forward and determine our happiness. We form a pure conscious sense of another person's character; and as to discussion of an issue, can find ourselves considering that more may be involved than meets the eye, that what we have been told may not be truth. Thought moves the body, and it is the pure subjective process that made a difference.

No mind in western civilization existed separate from exposure to Christian influence. Every aspect of social change is relative to something we realize deep within personal thought; to our humanity. People began to follow an inner guidance; completely subjective perceptions. This 'inner vision' became 'the way', replaced incompatible governing structures. Unlike poor Sisyphus, who reached the summit, only to fall back down, in likeness to 'old world' establishments, and the 'old world gods', who punished; the God we now envisioned, gave us a government, where we could not only reach the summit rapidly, but continue to unimaginable heights. The means seemed an envisagement of the natural intrinsic structure of both the physical body and environment.

The government of The United States of America is a simulation of the manner the physical world works, and was introduced long before this scientific knowledge became part of our reality. The overall arrangement is one where each cell matters; contributes to a unit; which contributes to a system; all contribute harmoniously toward the welfare of the whole;—and most noteworthy is the fact,—directional energy flows from the inside-out. The pattern is standard, evident in all natural and man-made animated objects. We need to consider whether the similarity in human creations, to the physical mechanism of our world; suggests our environment had a Creator, of which we hold a conscious likeness; or is the manner mankind creates, simply an adaptive mental mechanism to basic physical structure. This similarity of structure of the physical machine, to the way mankind creates could also suggest this creator may not have been God, but an original consciousness of man, from which we all have become almost an insignificant piece. We could wonder if that consciousness became dissociated, and each of us is a piece; or even if that consciousness sleeps, and we are but a dream. Somehow this relativity in creative style seems significant, holds some key toward enlightenment.

"I no more believe the universe was formed by a fortuitous concourse of atoms, than that the accidental jumbling of the alphabet would form a most ingenious treatise of philosophy."
—Jonathan Swift

This quote makes sense to me. If mankind is only a physical product, then like other life forms, should hold an intrinsic knowledge of its world. Were the similarity in creation style simply a biological connection; to express it should have been a spontaneous part of our natural course. It is evident the mind formed by the body was inhibitory to realization of a personal creative nature. The predator-prey like mentality formed by the environment is the reason it took thousands of years; revolutions, wars and personal social battles; until a government arrangement came into existence compatible with our true nature. We can consider the introduction of a system of law and order as an adaptive mechanism, in likeness to the steadfast laws governing the physical world. However it is important to note, that the system introduced by the physiological mind was incompatible. Instead laws evolve toward satisfying our common sense of fairness. Personal creative nature was masked by oppressive laws. FREEDOM of an individual, and our country from 'old world' thought was the law that activated personal ability. In actuality, the mind formed by body and environment conflicts with our true inherent conscious nature, inhibits realization of even physical truths, and satisfaction of all personal needs. To strain our mental soup may reveal we are not at all the physical creatures we believe ourselves to be.

The idea of physiological ascension seems somewhat paradoxical. Even though an organism may become more virulent through physical adaptation, it is going nowhere; will come to an end. We are so pre-occupied with physical objects, but it is consciousness that matters. Not only is personal consciousness where the object exists, and impacts us; but where we unite, become one with objects, or share the same world. Physical changes did not effect our awesome progress over the past three centuries. We changed our thinking; became guided not by eyesight; but insight. Human ascent was not a physiological evolution, but a conscious transcendence. Not the need for air, food and water; but desire for truth moved us forward. The only positive motion in our world seems the ever expanding consciousness of humanity. An occurrence made possible because knowledge, or a conscious world exists, which we have the capacity to perceive. At birth we enter not only a world of objects, but of thoughts as well. The energy of our ascent did not flow from objects, but from the manner an already existent common thought, impacted our deepest conscious senses. To consider the overall direction of humanity, we could only conclude that an inherent natural conscious affinity for truth was a primary instrument of navigation. That this is an instinctive drive also becomes apparent in that truths form a natural conformity; end conflict.

Our progress seems almost to suggest we do have an intrinsic knowledge of our environment, but have not been in our right mind. We seem to have been deceived by our physical senses. Human reality is an ever changing entity, because we find what was believed to be real,—is not! It is now evident that the mind originated by an isolated primitive human body; an image of environmental appearance and activity was inaccurate. This physical mind disguised the real environment. The manner truths entered our reality, suggests this mind also disguised the real person. We may not have established accurate reason as to why our remote ancestors were functioning below conscious capability. It could be more consideration needs to be given as to why the limitation for thousands of years, and then the sudden spurt of genius over the past century. We agree the answer surrounds the difference American government made. However where we credit the democratic format, something less visible may have been responsible. Before America, both the governing and governed were on automatic pilot; functioning through the physical senses. The physical mind was in control. Orders were written; people obeyed. Thomas Jefferson most especially expressed a far deeper vision. Social reform flowed with respect for fairness, and personal worth. Human ideals as equality, compassion, peace, truth, freedom or justice are pure conscious entities; can be found only within personal consciousness, or Self. So in essence, America may have restored humanity to a natural state; to a right mind. The Constitution removed people from oppressive physical control; to a far deeper Self-control; which success seems to have proven is our true consciousness.

The place we envision equality or justice; photosynthesis or gravity; or any physical principle is within personal consciousness. Truths are subjective; are not 'out there', but within personal consciousness. We tend to rely on physical analysis of the objective world as means to determine truth. Overlook the fact that the scientific method is a conscious process; happens within personal consciousness. The fact alone that personal consciousness has proved our most prized possession, and holds no scientific understanding should be evidence there is more to reality than the objective world. Still we focus on the body. We reveal the intrinsic structure of biological existence, including the physical mechanism of human anatomy and physiology. With minds firmly connected to the objective environment, we press forward. The knowledge is vital to our welfare. Then, is not personal consciousness, the source of that knowledge even more vital? We seem to disregard the fact that although organic physiology comes into view, the source of its life remains an enigma. The answer may remain occult unless we correct our vision. Consciousness is what determines our reality. We recognize the environment is not as it appears, but retain the primitive concept that the human body is the 'person'. Personal consciousness is what is real; seems to be the ONE truth, from which all our physical knowledge has derived. Realization of behavioral and physical truths brought us together in thought, as though we are instinctively moving toward one true world. Were directed by an inherent drive for personal need satisfaction, which our limited mentality, and the social reality so created, does not provide. Our ascent was not made possible by physical adaptation; but quite the opposite, personal freedoms from the mentality so acquired, and perpetuated by human authority. When we believed in a 'Loving Father' of humanity, who would always forgive, as long as we tried to adhere to the IDEAL behavior of His Son; we would find truth, "and the truth would set us free"; with heaven the eventuality;—that is exactly what was happening.

There is nothing in the message of Jesus to suggest it was intended for anything other than the whole of humanity; or is relative to anything other than a means to realize our true inheritance. We have an age-old academic division on the nature of truth. The fact that the word truth defies academic definition alone should be supporting evidence for subjectivity. Webster defines truth as "agreement with reality." This becomes of interest as it is evident humanity is still not in its right mind; has lost contact with reality. The mind formed by objects we perceived through the physical senses has been wrong. The world is not flat; to bleed someone is not the way to cure illness; nor was trephination, the opening of the skull to release evil spirits any indication of sanity. To say nothing of the burning of witches, the Catholic Inquisition; or the entire human master-slave affair. Many ancient ideas have been abandoned as steadfast truths arrive. The process of finding truth, or reality, seems far from complete. As we still are not certain of our origin, or destiny; it seems fair to consider human reality, may differ from true reality. Society adjusts as truths arrive, and many worlds, or realities have come and gone. That the revelation of steadfast truths is responsible for the impermanence of human reality, would suggest the truth is we are part of an everlasting world. Humanity may be part of an existence so awesome, it becomes indefinable through our still limited minds. The heaven we've craved in our hearts throughout all the changing realities may be right in our midst; the truth just awaits our realization.

Physical objects formed the foundation of our reality. The truths we have revealed are relative to that objective mind and world. So, we could consider these truths limited to human reality; or the physical mind-object interchange. It could be that we have only corrected our reality to the point of revealing human truths; or limited truth to proximal awareness. Academia has only elevated our thought a notch from automation; to promote exercise of a deeper reasoning capacity relative to the structure of objects. We can see that what interfered with realization of even physical truths are differences in individual points in time, space and person. Our course shows realization of behavioral ideals, and release of that mindset by American government was a precedent to our recent ascent. The mindset proved compatible with a common sense of right behavior, thus brought us together; decreased the dimensions of our separation. Then transportation improved, again bringing us together; decreasing the variation in mentality caused by separation as to time and place. Medical progress moved us toward a more common state of well-being, on which perception and contribution of knowledge is dependent. The science of psychology began to understand the physical mind, allowing us to better inter-relate. There is no question that to 'come together in thought' is an instinctive drive. There was always a tendency to conform, but truths allowed it to happen naturally. The greatest avenue of progress has been in communication. Technology has provided means for all to share knowledge; to reach an eventual truth, a unity of mind and body. We seem directed toward a world where no person is disconnected from reality.

There is another paradox we need to consider though if eventual contentment is to be our destination. Although objectivists seem to consider the physical world as an entity in existence separate from personal consciousness; they remain firmly connected to it. Common sense alone tells us the physical world existed before we experienced it; and does exist separate from our conscious awareness. However to me, this implies a person is somehow something separate from that physical existence. Like a traveler passing through a new city, that existed before arrival, and will continue after departure. All can agree what matters is the nature of the experience, and that is an entirely personal conscious sense. Despite similarity in physical structure, the experience of each person is unique; as is personal consciousness unique from other physical entities. It seems we would have to consider reality to be the objective world, because its realness is supported by factual information, and physical principles are steadfast truths. It is our perception of the environment that has been wrong, and also holds individual variation. Despite this though, further consideration may not eliminate the subjective view of reality. Our progress shows the mind formed by the objective world was incorrect; so it would be illogical to consider the real-idea mental mechanism; a sole explanation. This is often the case with realists, who in essence stay connected to the physical world by assuming we are only objects, produced by the environment; but provide no explanation of why our consciousness was dissociated from it; or why it would seem to exist separate from us.

It seems clear humanity has been separated from reality through conscious dissociation. Personal consciousness gets scattered all over the place. It attaches to appearances, to things, opinion of others, actions of animals, routines, to thoughts of the past and future, to actions of other people, to all sorts of environmental activity, social laws, theories, political activities—with the conglomeration becoming a physical mind, and a synthetic self develops; and the same with the consciousness of humanity. Jesus may have restored that chaotic conscious activity to its natural source. Through an awareness brought forth by parables, created an inner vacuum and pulled all that energy away from the environment back into the person, the true Self. He moved authority from religious and social leaders to God, to a place deep within personal thought. Jesus encouraged not religious ritual or ceremony, but personal prayer. His behavior, the manner He treated other people awakened perhaps vestigial images, as equality, peace, truth, freedom,—a memory of our capacity to love. These human ideals flowed like the energy in all living things, from the inside-out! Not from a human designated authority figure, but an exemplification from a carpenter, who walked around the countryside talking to people, somehow reached this inner vision. The message diffused throughout western civilization, and around the globe. The WORD is the composite of these intrinsic human ideals. The Law was a Golden Rule: "Do unto others, as you would have them do unto you." A completely subjective ideation emerged. The Word can't be defined or instructed; is ethereal, holds no physical source; exists only within personal consciousness. Having no physical identity, became labeled the 'human spirit'. This became the light of our world, the source of human decency and progress. Overcame what seemed overwhelming physical obstacles, and determined our course.

It must be considered the completely subjective mindset of common ethereal ideals is in fact also very real. These are the conscious energies that brought objective truths into view, utilized the knowledge and directed it toward common welfare. This seems evidence Jesus accomplished all that was necessary. He organized, or put personal consciousness in a natural order. The inner vision of each person is the same, but becomes expressed in diverse manners because of individual physical variation. Personal prayer somehow evoked a sense of personal responsibility to fulfill talent, and be concerned for the welfare of another person. That the Word is not only different, but an opposition to the mind acquired from the objective world, and predator-prey-physical activity; as everything in the human mind has a real source; can only suggest our subjective reality extends beyond the physical view to an entirely different conscious existence; which is reflected through personal consciousness. Essentially the message of Jesus detached our consciousness from objects, which began restoration of a highly resilient intact perfect SELF; which began a natural cohesion with each other; and God. Suggestion is human reality does not yet exist; but is in the making. There is no question only through the free conscious agents we call human IDEALS, can a compatible human reality be brought into existence; or that personal character recognition through meditation is the way.

The objective-subjective dilemma may simply reflect the opposition of body and consciousness. We love to see things grow, desire everlasting well-being; but view an environment where things come to an end. Conditions seem to be reversed; contrary to intrinsic conscious need, and necessary physical order. Compounded by the problem where the physical view has formed our minds, and assumed control. This seems contrary to a natural arrangement, which seems to be for consciousness to direct the body. The emphasis in the New Testament of the Bible seems to be on obedience to the Spirit within. With Jesus being the behavioral exemplification of when the "Word becomes flesh". Our direction toward truth and compatibility could have been perceived from a consciousness right in our midst; more may exist than the objective world, and human thought. One thing is clear, it is entirely personal subjective thought that makes a difference; introduces only positive and compatible changes, and seems capable of unlimited actualities. The people who made a difference were different; they were alive! 'The Way' to personal contentment and strength was considered to be 'invisible' by ancient Orientals, as Lao Tzu; and so has it proven to be for humanity. Indications are the Christian religious establishment misinterpreted the WORD. Still, the people understood. The subjective message of Jesus may have been best expressed by William Penn: "To mend the world is true religion."

I do not think we should abandon the Bible as holding an explanation for existence, and means of finding personal identity. To extend our thought beyond literal interpretation, and exercise our deeper reasoning capacity may be the need. The story of creation in Genesis could be a guide to truth. It could be that God brought man into existence, but that neither that man, nor that existence is anything like we have been taught to believe. Nor did God create man in the same limited manner we bring things into existence. The creation may somehow have been an extension of the consciousness of God, more God-like. Or God may have brought man into existence, and then that man brought the physical world into existence. We may see our resemblance to God, in our own desire to bring things into existence, and love to see life forms grow; or in our ethereal intrinsic ideals. Or our conscious likeness to original man may be evident in that all of our mechanical creations, and the most successful political format; are simulations of the intrinsic manner the physical world is arranged; where each unit matters, contributes to a system,— and all contribute harmoniously for the welfare of the whole; with energy flowing from the inside-out. The conscious connection may also be evident in the manner we find physical truths, and copy organic and physical principles and arrangements. The idea that original man could have created this world could be supported by the fact each individual creates a personal reality, and evidenced by the many social realities mankind has created. Or the physical world could be the manner in which "God clothed Adam and Eve" after their downfall that Genesis discusses. Temporal existence may be the manner in which Adam and Eve were limited, or removed from reality. Or the negative motion that moves things toward an end could have been caused by their conscious separation from God.

I, personally, am convinced we were brought into existence by a greater conscious being. We do not show evidence that we are physiological ascendants in that predation is incompatible to an inherent nature. The fact that consciousness has been the life of our body, of our world; and that the energy flowed from entirely subjective common intrinsic ideals is more suggestive we are ethereal descendants. Still, we must have been creations, because all indications are that true consciousness does not begin, but is an ever-existent entity; where in our case we are dependent on the body machine for conscious access; the physical body and world is our life-support machine. The consciousness accessed, or the 'invisible person' has no physical composition, and so most likely, even though had a beginning, becomes an everlasting entity. The 'invisible person' does have an ethereal composition, social needs which are compatible with the environment in its normal state, but not with the oppressive activity that causes harm and brings things to an end. This can only mean the negative motion was not part of an original reality. It is my suspicion we are descendants from an original man, which was an extension of the consciousness of God. Somehow there may have been a separation between man and God. This dissociated consciousness brought forth the negative energy. Structure suggests an original world where automatic body function was the only necessity for knowledge and contentment. After the "fall" instead the body accessed predatory activity, and enhanced the negative direction through the mind so acquired. To escape as indicated in Genesis, "we would have to become like Gods," which I believe has been the recent occurrence through the scientific discoveries relative to our deeper reasoning capacity.

The intrinsic structure of body, environment and human consciousness are all suggestive of original arrangement for infinite existence. The physical world is ever present, as is consciousness. We do not exist in the past or future, but only experience the present. The manner our consciousness expands is due to the existence of everlasting truths, and conscious ability to perceive them. We clearly have had a perceptual disorder. Our vision clears as we reach a greater conscious depth. We also may find reason to consider an everlasting consciousness is in our midst within consideration our predecessors did not perceive something visible, but knowledge; and the only place knowledge can exist is within consciousness. Everything within the physical realm is inter-related, including thought. Every thought in the human mind has a real source, whether or not the perception is accurate; and every human invention uses a real physical principle already in existence. We are not entirely authentic, but dependent on what is already in existence. There is no reason to suspect we are original objective creatures or subjective spirits. Our subjective authenticity is not without physical restraint. We are synthetic, have been functioning like copy machines. When we copy environmental actions, experience a reality where there is competition for power, coercion, war, inequality, bondage, hatred, greed, poverty, suffering, habitual robotic performance and injustice. We need to get out of this habit!

Jesus essentially initiated personal freedom from environmental control. When the environment forms the mind, images are of things past, applied to future concerns; which determine a behavioral response. This process is an automatic body function; requires no personal effort. Like the heart pumps blood, the brain forms thought; and thought moves the body. The thoughts of the people Jesus talked to were formed by objects, by physical appearance and activity. Human behavior in His era simulated the predator-prey style of animals. Society held a negative motion that causes harm, and brings things to an end. The environmental view reflects a world where pleasure is dependent on physical power. This simulation radiates from ancient worlds. The only way to determine who has the most physical power is to use force; and this always inflicts pain. We see this exercised throughout all the eras, with the only change being a decrease in the degree of brutality. To escape from this primitive mind formed by environmental appearance is our need. Retention of the basic concepts is the root of our unhappiness. Those who found this personal freedom showed us 'the way' can't be explained in words; is written only in our hearts. We appreciate their contributions, but are lost; return to insanity.

We scream for freedom, but it is futile. This is not something we can receive from the 'outside'. They do not have it to give.

Those with the most physical power have always ruled. In contrast to the obedience of the people to the Golden Rule, where the road to freedom resides; positions of power always remained exactly that. Rulers firmly adhere to the principle of coercion. The idea of personal freedom is not in their mindset. Everything physical is interrelated. There is no physical freedom. Freedom is not known by the mind formed by the physical environment. The only freedom possible is from erroneous thought, or by now we should be able to say from the primitive mind; because most of it has proven to be incorrect. We retain the primitive view pleasure is dependent on degree of physical power. This is what needs to be corrected, if freedom is to be realized. There can never be any freedom in a world where physical power is respected. There are no two people with equal physical strength. One person has more power than another. A hierarchy arrangement based on physical power gives one person power over another, with the overall effect inhibitory to the freedom of all, with variance only in degree.

Nature has given us an instinctive drive for freedom, but obviously it is not a physiological endowment. Freedom is a pure conscious idea, has no earthy source. Therefore it can only be satisfied within consciousness, and the manner is to detach oneself from the constant flow of environmental thoughts that flood our minds. To free the SELF, and restore its natural position is our need. Then severed from physical restraint, a person can expend the unlimited conscious energy; become the free agent nature intended. This could have been the implication when Jesus said the need is to 'give up everything, and follow Him'. The message was all about consciousness; about SELF identity. The impact of His teachings is evident in the personal character strengths that began to emerge throughout western civilization.

THE LONG OVERDUE LETTER

To a people, whose minds were almost entirely formed and controlled by environmental stimuli, came a visible human physical form, whose mind was not so formed. This person explained, and demonstrated what marvelous abilities are within us. He really got their attention when "He arose from the dead". Every lesson He gave seems to surround the way to find personal freedom from physical limitations. When social conformity supported guidance from God through personal prayer, we assumed a positive direction, made astounding progress. Because human thought is dominated by physical images, and the physical world is regulated by exact laws; we tend to make everything concrete and structured. Religions probably can't unite for the same reason. They try to define, and set rigid rules to something that can't be defined in human terms; can't be limited or restricted,—something entirely subjective called PERFECT LOVE.

I'll close with that thought. Many days have passed since I started to reminisce. Thoughts continue to flood my mind. There is no end. We could go on forever. So much distracts us from what really matters. This we can only find in our hearts. Here there is no separation. Life is a "Sentimental Journey."

There is a lot of talk about the need for change among the Presidential candidates. Our founders may have made the only change necessary. We may have failed to recognize it. The Constitution they framed is a work of art. A door to continuous growth and everlasting happiness was opened for us. The only deterrent seems the 'American Dream' remained encapsulated in the ancient materialistic mindset. The American Constitution is almost perfect, should never be changed. These men were short-sighted in one area though. What they failed to imagine was a future where personal relationship to God was not paramount.

This unpredictable occurrence almost makes interpretation of their thoughts impossible. Our Constitution seems a framework to support personal ethereal ideals. The mindset of equality, truth, freedom, peace, love and justice exists only in our hearts. They are not of this world; not of the reality brought into existence by mankind!

We seem to have taken a necessary detour. To enhance the intellectual machine is a vital necessity. Current conditions though suggest we need to get back on the right course. The master-slave affair is again intensifying. It seems vital we end the masquerade. Personal consciousness has proved to be the true intelligence. Our Declaration of Independence implies the intent of our founders was for us to follow a course determined by "Nature, and Nature's God." We have an intrinsic mechanism to guide our behavior; an inherent social conscience. The problem seems meditation is the only way to identify, and release it. The freedom given in America may have been from the basic mentality of mankind which has always dominated our thought. Our ascension may be entirely related to their allowance for personal proximity to God.

> May we help our children find;
>   a place where all are teachers and students;
>   and the lesson is love.

CPSIA information can be obtained at www.ICGtesting.com
224432LV00001B/34/P